THE WISDOM OF THE WORD
FAITH

THE WISDOM OF THE WORD

FAITH

Great African-American Sermons

EDITED BY

Rhinold Ponder
and Michele Tuck-Ponder
Foreword by Reverend Samuel D. Proctor
Illustrations by Bruce Waldman

CROWN PUBLISHERS, INC.
NEW YORK

Grateful acknowledgment is made to the following for permission to reprint previously published material:

"What Man Lives By" by Benjamin E. Mays, from *Best Black Sermons*, William M. Philpot, ed. (Valley Forge, PA: Judson Press, 1972), pp. 31–39. Reprinted with permission of the publisher, Judson Press, 1-800-458-3766. "Prayer" from *Challenge* by Louis Untermeyer, copyright 1914 by Harcourt Brace & Company and renewed 1942 by Louis Untermeyer. Reprinted by permission of the publisher. "A Storm-Proof Religion" by Gardner C. Taylor. Reprinted by permission of the author. "Faith: What It Is and What It Does" by Dr. J. Alfred Smith, Jr., Senior Pastor, Allen Temple Baptist Church. Reprinted by permission of the author. "Tempt God" by Howard Thurman. Reprinted by permission of the Howard Thurman Educational Trust. Thirty-three lines from "The Rich Young Ruler" by Clive Samson. Reprinted by permission of David Higham Associates. "Talking to a Dead Man" by Rev. Dr. A. Safiyah Fosua. Reprinted by permission of the author. "Moving from Endangerment to Empowerment" by Rev. Raymond Lee Harris, Jr., Associate Pastor, St. Anthony of Padua/Most Precious Blood Church. Reprinted by permission of the author. "Strange Deliverance" by H. Beecher Hicks, Jr. Reprinted by permission of Kerygma Associates, Inc. on behalf of the author. "Stewards of the Mysteries" by William Augustus Jones, Jr. Reprinted from *Responsible Preaching* by permission of the author. "God Is Faithful When We Fail" by Harold Dean Trulear, Ph.D., Professor of Church and Society, New York Theological Seminary. Reprinted by permission of the author.

Copyright © 1996 by Ponder Literary Properties, Inc.

Illustrations copyright © 1996 by Bruce Waldman

Published by Crown Publishers, Inc., 201 East 50th Street, New York, New York 10022. Member of the Crown Publishing Group.

Random House, Inc. New York, Toronto, London, Sydney, Auckland

http://randomhouse.com/

CROWN is a trademark of Crown Publishers, Inc.

Printed in the United States of America

Design by Julie Duquet

Library of Congress Cataloging-in-Publication Data is available upon request

ISBN 0-517-70591-5

10 9 8 7 6 5 4 3 2

First Edition

CONTENTS

ACKNOWLEDGMENTS

The great works compiled in this volume could not have been gathered without the support and cooperation of numerous individuals, many of whom, through their efforts, treated this project as their own.

We would like to express our deepest gratitude to Rev. Reginald T. Jackson, pastor of St. Matthew's A.M.E. Church in Orange, New Jersey; Dr. Peter Paris of Princeton Theological Seminary, New Jersey; Dr. Jeremiah A. Wright, Jr., pastor of Trinity United Church of Christ in Chicago; Dr. Cleo LaRue of the New Brunswick Theological Seminary, New Jersey; and Dr. Gerald Davis. Their efforts in identifying some of America's greatest messengers of the Word and their advice about evaluating these works were invaluable.

We offer special thanks to Rosalyn Andrews, Rev. Warren Dennis, Charles Hardaway, Adrienne Ingrum, Dr. Calvin Morris, and Minnie Wright of the Interdenominational Theological Center in Atlanta, and to Dr. Dolly A. McPherson, Lillie Webb-McPherson, Dr. Alvin Ponder, III, Dr. Russell Adams, and Bishop Prince Taylor. Each of them played a special and essential role in shaping this project.

We extend a special acknowledgment to our staff—Angelique Harris, Sharahn Thomas, and Ava Gascer—for their dedication and hard work.

Great thanks and blessings to Carol Taylor, our editor, who had the insight and foresight to see the need for this historical and spiritual undertaking.

Of course, we offer our love and eternal gratitude to our parents, William A. Tuck and the late Anna M. Tuck and Carrie B. Ponder, who have loved us and prepared us for the possibilities of our own good.

And most important, our thanks to God, who makes all things possible.

FOREWORD
by
Reverend Samuel D. Proctor

THIS IS AN ambitious undertaking, and one that will reap rich rewards, both in personal, spiritual benefits as well as in altering the moral tone of our communities. It is an effort to gather the harvest of the most creative, well-prepared, and committed servants of the Word, and make their gifts available to a wider audience.

It is tricky business grading preachers. One imposes on God's will and God's design one's own narrow grasp of what is a touch of the divine. Yet, this is where we are, finite creatures always skirting the boundaries of the infinite, temporal limitations in confrontation with the infinite. And with the clear understanding, these sermons are endorsed and recommended for the serious reader.

One may expect to experience a kind of audit, an inventory of your own spiritual equipment. Good sermons are searching.

One may further expect an awakening to our social and economic pathologies, a challenge to our compassion and our understanding of justice and fairness.

One may also experience an inhaling of a spiritual elixir, an aroma of the good news, a refreshing of the soul, a glimpse of eternity, for good sermons have no limit in their element of surprise. Remember, it is not only the preacher looking up, but God looking down, and in spite of our earnestness, God is greater, wiser, more loving, and more intentional about effecting a God-human reconciliation. Watch for that.

Amen.

Introduction

THE SEARCH FOR spiritual guidance and inspiration has recently experienced a resurgence in American society, particularly among African Americans. After two decades of movement away from the traditional black church and its theological teachings, we are now witnessing the beginning of a spiritual "homecoming" for African Americans.

For some, the journey to spiritual fulfillment has begun with a return to communal worship. For others, the journey involves a personal exploration of a variety of sources of wisdom, including the Bible, but also incorporating such diverse spiritual writings as the Koran, the Torah, and any number of writings by theologians, ministers, teachers, and other spiritualists. But for most of us, the foundation of religious or spiritual study remains in the black church, with the primary source being the pastor's interpretation of the Bible as it reveals the Word of God.

The Wisdom of the Word reflects the expressive oral tradition cultivated in the black church, as well as the rich quality of theological interpretation and spiritual insight. As we shaped this volume, we were concerned that one of the most important features of African-American preaching—the compelling oral delivery and style—might be lost. However, the process of selecting these pieces corrected us on two counts. First, the most outstanding feature of black preaching is its content, not its style. The Word of God dictates all in this context, and style is merely a communicative vehicle. Second, the style of black homiletic oratory varies greatly among the clergy and, in significant part, oral styles can be captured on the printed page. Readers will appreciate the differ-

11

ences, for instance, between the intellectual grace of Howard Thurman and the heavenly cadence of Gardner C. Taylor.

Also intriguing are the different ways each messenger treats the theme of faith and the variety of illustrative ways their points are delivered. In one sermon, H. Beecher Hicks, Jr., successfully accepts the difficult task of explaining how God's methods of delivering us from oppression may seem strange to us, but are actually designed to secure our total faith and understanding. In A. Safiyah Fosua's sermon, we are challenged to understand that faith leads to resurrection from the living dead. The variety of treatment of the topic is both intriguing and masterful.

We must make one other important point. These sermons are not only for African Americans. Just as God touches us all as members of humanity, these sermons contain important messages for people of all colors. After all, our point is that the Word is to be exalted and passed on to those seeking a closer relationship with truth and faith.

These are great sermons, by some of our community's greatest preachers, selected for their strength, thoughtfulness, and clarity, and for their relevance to our daily lives. These sermons breathe life into the Word, thereby making the Bible real and relevant to our everyday existence. We are proud to make this offering to you. We pray that you are as enriched and blessed by these words of wisdom, joy, worship, and faith as we have been.

WHAT MAN LIVES BY
Benjamin E. Mays

We are reminded that Man does not live by bread alone,
but by the word of God. Man must live by
faith in God and himself.

MATTHEW 4:4

SOME NINETEEN CENTURIES ago a Palestinian Jew made these words immortal: "Man shall not live by bread alone, but by every word that proceedeth out of the mouth of God" (Matthew 4:4, King James Version). To state it another way: Man shall not live by bread alone but by every good thing that God provides. Man can *exist* on food, air, and water, just as animals can, but man must have more than bread in order to live creatively and constructively.

It is not too much to translate this passage by saying, Man shall not live by material things alone. Money, houses and land, stocks and bonds, silver and gold, iron and ore, silks and diamonds and pearls and furs are all important, but man may have all these and merely exist—not live.

Jesus stated it wisely: Man shall not live by bread alone. He knew that bread—food—is basic to man's life. And the Devil knew that when a man gets hungry, he is vulnerable and may do many abnormal things in order to get food. Facing starvation, most people would steal, if they could, rather than starve. Using bread as a symbol for food, adequate food for all mankind has been a problem since the beginning of time. It is a crucial problem today. It is estimated that half the people of the earth are starving for lack of bread. Bread is so important that if food became too scarce, the strong man would turn on the weak man and cannibalize him in order to survive. The population-explosion threat is no idle dream. If bread becomes too unobtainable, we have the basis for revolution. In man's quest for more bread—more food—and a higher standard of living, labor strikes against management and the common people rise up against the establishment. Those of us who care are appalled by the fact that easily thirty million Americans are living below the poverty line. Bread is important, and man cannot exist without it. But if man had only food, only material things, to live by, he would cease to be a man.

So Jesus says to the Devil that man cannot live by bread alone.

If he could, he would be a mere animal. Bread is the means, not the end. Man lives in God, and the circumference of life cannot be rightly drawn until the center is set. Carlyle said that "not all the finance ministers and upholsterers and confectioners of modern Europe in joint stock company" could "make one shoeblack happy . . . above an hour or two." If bread and material things were the sine qua non of life, the rich and the affluent would be eternally happy and the less rich would be eternally miserable. But history records, and experience reveals, that some of the most miserable people are among those who have great wealth and those who have achieved fame.

The experience of Jesus in the wilderness is common to all mankind. Simply put, Jesus is trying to decide the basic question that confronts every man: What shall I do with my life? This question faces every man: What shall I do with my life? Although I shall deal with only one of the three temptations, Jesus is getting his priorities straight. Man has to decide what he will put first in his life. This problem faces the young with terrific force. If it is money, material wealth, houses and land, stocks and bonds, silver and gold—as important as these are—if these are central in our lives, human values become secondary. Man may exist, but he will never know the full joy of living. As indispensable as bread is, as vital as material things are, possessions alone have never made a man great. The rich man who achieves a degree of greatness achieves it not because he hoards his wealth but because he gives it away in the interest of good causes—his concern for humanity, his concern for the poor, and his desire to improve the quality of education. The truly great men of history are great not because of the abundance of the things they possessed but because of their dreams and the contributions they made to mankind. It is because they recognized that man cannot live by bread alone.

Many years ago, H. G. Wells named the six great men of history. He named Buddha and Aśoka, brown men; Aristotle, a Greek; Roger Bacon, an Englishman; Abraham Lincoln, an American; and the greatest among them, Jesus, a Jew. If I were to name my list, I would want to include men like Albert Schweitzer, Mahatma Gandhi, and my pupil and friend, Martin Luther King,

Jr. These men knew that man cannot live by bread alone but by every word that proceedeth out of the mouth of God.

Bread is vital; it is indispensable; but in appraising a man for greatness, wealth per se is never a criterion. Nobody stops to ask how much wealth persons like Fred Douglass, Harriet Tubman, Thomas Aquinas, Albert Einstein, Booker T. Washington, Mary McLeod Bethune, Shakespeare, and Socrates had when they died. They achieved historical immortality long after bread ceased to sustain their bodies. If man cannot live by bread alone, what else does he need to live by? Jesus answers this by saying: By every word that proceedeth out of the mouth of God.

Any man or woman who has a family knows that man lives by affection and love. There may be material things galore, but if there is no affection, no love in the home, the family falls apart. The baby may have all the food it needs, all the air and sunshine, all the protection from cold and heat; yet if he does not get his mother's kisses, her affectionate hugs, her inviting smiles, and her soothing words when he cries, the baby may exist but he will be an abnormal child. The baby must be made to know that he or she is wanted. The child must have the love of father, mother, sisters, and brothers, and the protection they give—all these the child must receive in order to live and flourish.

No man has ever made his wife really happy merely by giving her an abundance of material things. He may give her gold and silver, diamonds and pearls, houses and land, stocks and bonds—all these she will reject if her husband withholds his love. In truth, love is the thing no man or woman can live without. Affection and love hold the family together; hatred and infidelity tear the family apart. Man cannot live by bread alone. Bread must be accompanied by love and affection.

No man can live without forgiveness. The family cannot hold together without it. The husband and wife must forgive each other for the unkind words they sometimes say to each other, for the unpleasant glances they sometimes give, for being impatient with one another. Even if at times husband and wife are deliberately mean toward one another, they must forgive. Forgiveness is the very essence of happiness in the home. The family cannot survive if the wife seeks opportunities to get revenge for unkind things the husband says and does to her. Nor can the family hold together if the husband seeks retaliation against the wife. Forgiveness is the heart of family life. The father must forgive the son, the son the father; the sister must forgive her brother and the brother the sister; the wife must forgive the husband and the husband the wife. I have even known cases where there was forgiveness where infidelity was involved. It takes a lot of forgiveness to keep a family together.

Man must live by forgiveness, not only family forgiveness but community forgiveness. The prisoner who served his time needs community forgiveness. Man needs forgiveness for the dirty, vicious things that some do to others. How often have we in some little or big way trespassed against a brother? We live by forgiveness of those friends who love us and stick with us though we sin against them.

But most of all, we live by the forgiveness of God. No man is perfect enough, no man is good enough not to need the forgiveness of God. In one sense we are all sinners. If a sinner is one who sins, we all qualify as sinners. All of us sometimes sin. If it is true that when we sin against man, we sin against God; when we lie to man, we lie to God; when we exploit man, we exploit God; when we hate man, we hate God—God must indeed be a forgiving God with man sinning against him all of the time! Man shall not live by bread alone, but man shall live and does live by the forgiveness of a merciful God.

In addition to bread, man lives by the grace of God. One definition of grace is that we get what we do not deserve. Every man who is honest with himself knows of instances when he got what he did not deserve, certainly that which he did nothing to achieve. God sends his rain on the just and the unjust. The moon and the sun shine on us all. The unrighteous live as long as the righteous. The best man does not always get the job. We often get honors and prizes which we have not earned. Someone dies and leaves us a bit of wealth which we never turned a little finger to get. The man we do not like sometimes does us a favor, to our embarrassment. We inherit a good mind by some means we do not understand, a mind which we did nothing to get. We develop into a handsome boy or beautiful girl by nature and nature's God, but we did nothing to get the beauty or the comeliness. Some are born into better circumstances than others, but we are not responsible for where we are born, nor for what we are born with. In some degree, we all get what we do not deserve, and we live by the grace of God.

Man shall not live by bread alone. Man must live by faith — faith in himself and faith in others. However beastly man may be, we must believe in him and rely on him. We trust the doctor to operate on our bodies. We trust the man who drives the automobile. We trust the banks to keep our money. We trust the man who directs us to an unfamiliar place. We trust the pilot who takes us three thousand feet above the ground. We live by faith in others. But most of all we must live by faith in ourselves — faith to believe that we can develop into useful men and women. No man can live without faith in himself — a sense of inner security. A child must learn early to believe that he is somebody worthwhile and that he can do many praiseworthy things. Without this hope, there would be nothing for him to do but commit suicide. Furthermore, man could not live hopefully without believing that he counts for something in this world. The greatest damage that the white man did to the black man through slavery and segregation was to beat him down so much that millions of Negroes believed that they were nobody. The hopelessness and despair of so many black youths today lie in the fact that they have never believed that they have dignity and worth as human beings. If the emphasis on blackness and black awareness today means that black people are beginning to be proud of their heritage and proud of being what they are — black — apologizing to no one, not even to God, for what they are, it is a good thing. Man lives best by a belief that he is somebody, God's creature, and that he has status not given to him by man but given to him by God.

Man must believe that however hard the road, however difficult today, tomorrow things will be better. Tomorrow may not be better, but we must believe that it will be. Wars may never cease, but we must continue to strive to eliminate them. We may not abolish poverty, but we must believe that we can provide bread enough to spare for every living creature and that we can find the means to distribute it. We may not exterminate racism, but we must believe that different racial groups can live together in peace, and we must never cease to try to build a society in which the fatherhood of God and the brotherhood of man become realities.

In other words, many must live by faith in God—faith to believe that God sustains good and not evil, peace and not war, truth and not lies, justice and not injustice, integrity and not dishonesty, the faith that [Robert] Browning talks about in "Epilogue" when he says:[1]

> One who never turned his back but marched breast
>   forward,
> Never doubted clouds would break,
> Never dreamed, though right were worsted, wrong would
>   triumph,
> Held we fall to rise, are baffled to fight better,
> Sleep to wake.

Not by bread alone but by the labors of others. No man is self-sustaining. We are dependent on the labors of many hands for the food we eat, for the clothes we wear, for the cars and planes in which we ride, for the books we read, for the teachers who teach us, for the skill of the surgeon, for the technical training of the pilot. We are dependent on the postman who brings the mail, on the controllers who guide the planes in and out of airports, and on the sanitation workers who take away the garbage. Our lives are interlaced, interwoven, and intertwined with the lives of all classes of men, and whether we like it or not we all need each other and every man is our brother.

Man shall not live by bread alone, but man must live by his dreams, by the goals he strives to reach, and by the ideals which he chooses and chases. What is man anyway? Man is flesh and blood, body and mind, bones and muscle, arms and legs, heart and soul, lungs and liver, nerves and veins—all these and more make a man. But man is really what his dreams are. Man is what he aspires to be. He is the ideals that beckon him on. Man is the integrity that keeps him steadfast, honest, true. If a young man tells me what he aspires to be, I can almost predict his future.

It must be borne in mind, however, that the tragedy in life does not lie in not reaching your goal. The tragedy lies in having no goal to reach. It isn't a calamity to die with dreams unfulfilled, but it is a calamity not to dream. It is not a disaster to be unable to capture your ideal, but it is a disaster to have no ideal to capture. It is not a disgrace not to reach the stars, but it is a disgrace to have no stars to reach for. Not failure, but low aim is the sin. Harriet du Autermont has beautifully said:[2]

> No vision and you perish;
> No ideal, and you're lost;
> Your heart must ever cherish
> Some faith at any cost.
>
> Some hope, some dream to cling to,
> Some rainbow in the sky,
> Some melody to sing to,
> Some service that is high.

To state it another way, man must live by some unattainable goal, some goal that beckons him on, but a goal so lofty, so all-embracing that it can never be attained. In poetry it is expressed in many ways. Browning expresses it when speaking of Andrea del Sarto:

> Ah, but a man's reach should exceed his grasp,
> Or what's a heaven for?

[James Russell] Lowell says it in his "L'Envoi to the Muse":[3]

> Just, just beyond, forever burn
> Gleams of a grace without return;
> Upon thy shade I plant my foot,
> And through my frame strange raptures shoot;

All of thee but thyself I grasp;
I seem to fold thy luring shape,
And vague air to my bosom clasp,
Thou lithe, perpetual Escape!

The unattainable ideal is beautifully expressed by [Ralph
Waldo] Emerson in his "Forerunners":[4]

Long I followed happy guides,
I could never reach their sides;
Their step is forth, and, ere the day
Breaks up their leaguer, and away.
Keen my sense, my heart was young,
Right good-will my sinews strung,
But no speed of mine avails
To hunt upon their shining trails.
On and away, their hasting feet
Make the morning proud and sweet;
Flowers they strew, — I catch the scent;
Or tone of silver instrument
Leaves on the wind melodious trace;
Yet I could never see their face.

[Louis] Untermeyer says it best in his poem "Prayer":[5]

God, though this life is but a wraith,
Although we know not what we use,
Although we grope with little faith,
Give me the heart to fight — and lose.

Ever insurgent let me be,
Make me more daring than devout;
From sleek contentment keep me free,
And fill me with a buoyant doubt.

Open my eyes to visions girt
With beauty, and with wonders lit —

But let me always see the dirt,
And all that spawn and die in it.

Open my ears to music; let
Me thrill with Spring's first flutes and drums —
But never let me dare forget
The bitter ballads of the slums.

From compromise and things half-done,
Keep me, with stern and stubborn pride;
And when, at last, the fight is won,
God, keep me still unsatisfied.

Man shall not live by bread alone. Man must live by affection and love; by forgiveness — forgiveness of man and the forgiveness of God; by God's grace; by the labors of many hands; by faith — faith in himself, faith in others, and faith in God. And finally man must live by his dreams, his ideals, the unattainable goal, and what he aspires to be. Man shall not live by bread alone.

WHAT I AM talking about today is a "storm-proof religion." We need a faith that is stress-resistant; that is able to stand difficulty. This pulpit is not interested in a gospel that works only inside these walls. I have called such a "hothouse faith."

Such a plant can survive, and maybe thrive, as long as the temperature is kept moderate and constant. It cannot stand shifts in the temperature. That is no faith worth having. And, if our Christianity means nothing more to us than that, then we need to look for some other way, or we need to look for THE WAY, because we have not found it. Our faith needs to be able to stand stress.

I do not know how many people I have seen come into this church. At first, they seemed so enthusiastic, so exuberant, so eager and they blossom so rapidly, flourish so much, are so active and then in one way or another the temperature changes. They had a reverse in life. Some disappointment came to them. Things did not turn out as they thought they were going to turn out. And they wilted and collapsed. Or somebody said something to them, or they thought somebody said something about them. And they could not stand it. Or to use my figure of speech, the contrary wind capsized the boat. And what happened to them I do not know. They were last seen foundering and floundering, without anything to hold on to.

You can test your faith by whether or not it can stand stress when things do not go as you figured they would; something happens that upsets your plans; you have to alter your strategy, get a new game plan. If you collapse, your faith is lacking. I remember when the 747s first came out. I remember the apprehensiveness all of us had about these giant things. We read they were to hold three hundred people in one airplane. In order to allay the apprehensiveness of the flying public, the manufacturer of those huge things spread far and wide the word that they had had test pilots carry these things into the air, carrying more weight than they would ever carry in normal flight. They were tested under the most adverse conditions and found able to stand stress. When a

A STORM-PROOF RELIGION
Gardner C. Taylor

We must have religion steeped in faith which can withstand the stress of life's tribulations. We can build a storm-proof religion by having Jesus in our life, talking to the Lord through constant prayer and listening to Jesus' message.

MATTHEW 8:23–27; MARK 4:35–41

plane was miraculously saved in Hawaii sometime ago, the claim was that what went wrong was stress. Metal fatigue sheared the metal, cut it in two. The whole top of the thing went off.

We need a storm-proof religion.

Suppose I were to tell you today that I have come with the formula that will allow you to have a religion that is storm-proof? There is no more wonderful word that I could ever speak to you than that we have a prescription for a religion that can stand stress, handle a storm, will not capsize, will not go under in heavy waters. That's what we need—religion that can stand stress and does not collapse and break up when things go wrong. That's what anybody needs who is going to live anytime at all in a world like this.

I want to follow an incident. It happens in the Gospel of Matthew in the eighth chapter. You'll find a companion passage in the Gospel of Mark in the fourth chapter. The Lord having taught, says to his disciples, "Let us go over to the other side," for the command of life is to always keep moving. You cannot stand still—anybody's religion that is immobilized is soon paralyzed. If you are not growing in grace, you are calcifying in faith. To stand still is to go back. Oh, to be sure, there are moments and seasons in life when we cannot press forward as we did once, but to settle down at any level of Christian growth is to spoil the whole business. A still church is a stagnant church. It does not have freshness moving through it. It does not have life. And the stillest thing you've ever seen is the thing you want least to be. Do you know what that is? Death is still, does not move, does not wrinkle any dresses, does not get any neckties askew. It is an awful stillness.

The Lord Jesus says to his disciples, "Let us go over to the other side." The Lord is always calling his people forward. "Continue in my love," he says in the Gospel of John as he is about to depart. Don't quit. Keep moving. Oh my God, how as Christians we need to keep growing. There is so much we have not reached yet. God has worlds waiting on us, far more wonderful than anything we have experienced, if we will obey and keep going. "Follow me," he says. After he cured a man, he said, "You go. Don't stay here. Go back home. Tell your people what the Lord has done for you. Let us go over to the other side."

He was talking about the Sea of Galilee, which is an inland sea. Six or seven miles they were to travel across the Sea of Galilee. An inland sea can be as furious as, and perhaps more furious than, the open sea, because the open sea has such width to spread its turbulence. But an inland sea, like the Sea of Galilee, is confined, usually within mountains. I remember preaching in Central Africa years ago in what is now Malawi. A man named Oliver Ransford has written about the most captivating thing in that cold section of old Central Africa. He described how it can change moods. He said that sometimes by day it is so calm, the lake is like a tilted mirror to catch the languid artistry of the sky—the reflection of the sky in the water. Then, he said, at evening, the mood of Lake Malawi changes, its color becomes a purple; and then by night, when it is calm and the moon is shining upon it, it is a thing of beauty, of gold. But, it is located between two mountains and sometimes the winds that gather back up in the hills come screaming, come funneled, driven into an awful fury by their closeness of being limited by the walls of mountains. And the winds come with great fury. And then it becomes an awful frothing thing, sometimes with waves fifteen feet high. Well, that is what Galilee is like.

It is an inland sea. There are mountains, and sometimes when the winds come screaming through they meet in a concentrated fury and they set that sea into an awful frothing foam. You see, life gives us conditions and we cannot tell what winds we are going to meet. They form somewhere back in the mountains, out of our view. And when they get to us, they are already formed, they are already at work, they are already rushing through. The only air we can control is by fans and electricity, but the great winds that come at us come from elsewhere.

That night the Sea of Galilee was at first calm and placid, as they traveled that six or seven miles to the other side. Suddenly the winds came screaming down through the pass of the mountains. This sea, that had been so calm, became angry, frothing at the mouth, whitecapped waves billowing and dipping. And the little ship was bouncing and dipping in the trough of the waves until the disciples were horrified. Now you must take notice of this. The people who were on that ship were not land lovers; they were seafaring people. They were fishermen. They knew the Sea of Galilee. They had fished on it. It was their profession, their business. But on that particular occasion, the fury of the storm was so great that it terrified them.

Now, there was but one thing that that little ship, tossing upon this mad and angry sea, had—it had Jesus on board. That's the first element in this formula for a storm-proof religion: Jesus was on board. And, if you are going to handle this business we call life, this voyage, this sea, you need the Lord on board. I tell you this day that I would not go out of these doors—in fact I would not want to stay inside here with all of you here—without the Lord on board. Who can tell what is going to happen, what threats, what dangers are all around us?

> You mean to tell me you are willing to walk these streets without the Lord?
> You mean to tell me that you will get on these subways without the Lord?
> You mean to tell me that you will contract a marriage without the Lord?
> You mean to tell me that you will go into a hospital to be operated on and you don't have the Lord?
> You mean to tell me that you will enter into a business transaction and you don't have Jesus on board?
> My God, what a fool you must be! You and I need the Lord on our side!

Young people, you need the Lord on board. The sea is treacherous and dangerous. It's filled not only with natural dangers but with many pirates that will rob your ship.

They had the Lord on board. There is no use in talking about anything else. There is no use in discussing how to win friends and influence people. There is no use in arguing with you about how to make your life successful. If you do not have this first ingredient in the formula—if you don't have the Lord—you can't make it right. If you have the Lord on board, you're in good condition.

When the storm got furious—the lightning flashing, the great

thunder drums rolling, the wind screaming, and the waves thrash-
ing—these experienced seamen were terrified. They made their
living, before they joined Jesus, on the Sea of Galilee. But they
had never seen a storm like this, and having him on board they
had sense enough to call him.

That's the second ingredient: when things happen in your life,
you need enough presence of mind to call him. I do not know any
other way to make this journey except to call on the Lord. There is
no substitute for prayer. You and I can go over all the books on
self-help and self-culture and how to improve our minds and vocabulary, but unless we learn the vocabulary of prayer we are in a
bad fix. I am not talking now about only when just mild things
happen. I'm talking about when great winds blow contrary in
your life, you need to know how to call the Lord. Ask him to help
you. Talk to him. Plead with him. Ask the Savior to help you. He
is willing to heed you. He will carry you through. Oh my God, be
thankful for the privilege of going to him in prayer and presenting
before him our needs and telling him what our trouble is and what
has gone wrong in our lives. Thank God for the privilege of asking
him to protect our families and to take care of our children, to see
about our hopes, to handle our needs, to correct our faults, to con-
firm us in our faith, to strengthen us in our determination, to give
us the power to overcome, to stand the storm, to go on to see what
the end will be. This is what we need. We ought to talk regularly
to the Lord about our needs. It ought not be a brier-covered path
that we have to cross to get to the Lord. It ought to be a well-worn
path so that we don't need a road map to find where the Lord is.
We oughta travel that road so regularly that we can run hastily to
meet him, tell him our trouble. When trouble is upon you, you
don't have time to pick your way through thickets. You need right
then to be able to talk with him, to ask him to help. You need,
therefore, my brothers and sisters, to cultivate the prayer habit. I
don't mean just an empty habit. I mean to cultivate constant regu-
lar practice of being before God in prayer.

If you go to him when things are calm, you will find it easier in
the storm to talk to him. You won't have to work your way
through layers of difficulty, objections, qualifications, and uncer-

tainties. If you've been talking with him, you can talk with him more easily when trouble comes.

That's the second ingredient. They called out, "Master, carest thou not that we perish. The storm is raging. We are unable to handle it. These waves are mounting up. They are frothing at the mouth, a great and mighty tempest is blowing on this sea and it looks like we are momentarily going down. It seems as if this ship cannot last any longer. Master, carest though not that we perish."

They found the Lord asleep—not the sleep of indifference, but sleeping partly because he was weary. Sleeping also because he knew what to do. Panic comes because of frustration. No one ever gets into a panic who knows what the next step is. We go to pieces because we don't know what to do next. There is no condition in life so bad if we know the next step. He knew what the next step was. He was asleep and it was a sign of his identification with his humanity. I like that about our Lord. I am glad that he got tired and weary, because when we are tired and weary, he knows what it is all about. Because he's traveled the road that we have traveled. He's sweated our sweat, drunk our water, eaten our food, felt our loneliness, and suffered our sense of desertion. He knows all about our troubles. He's been this way, traveled this road. He knows all about your troubles.

> He knows where the road dips down.
> He knows where the currents are.
> He knows when the way is rough and rocky.
> He knows when it looks like your way is blocked and you cannot make it another step.
> He knows what it is to feel weariness.

And so, he slept. He slept also because there was in our Lord a great and wondrous and mysterious and inexplicable combination of the divine and the human. He slept as a human. He got up as divine. And we see that over and over again in his life, that strange mixture of what was mortal and was God himself. Have I ever told you how he wept at Lazarus' tomb? That was a man. But when he spoke, he spoke as a god and said, Lazarus come forth. It took a man to weep, but a god to speak. So he slept. And they shook him and said, "Master, carest thou not that we perish?"

I can see him now as he shakes the cobwebs of slumber from his eyes, stretches, and stands up to see the sea. Matthew did not hear what he said. Matthew says that he looked out into the sea and rebuked it. I don't know if Matthew quite grasped what the Lord said, but the sea knew who was looking at it. Mark said that Jesus said something and Mark heard what he said. He said, "Peace be still." I don't think it was a loud voice. I don't think it had to be, because the sea had heard that voice before, in the morning of creation, when he said, "Let there be." So the sea was not unacquainted with the voice that it heard when he said, "Peace be still." Dr. Goodspeed translates this into "Hush," like a mother talking to a child.

HUSH. The lightning folded its flame and ran back to its hiding place.

HUSH. The winds got still and fled to their homes in the hills.

HUSH. HUSH. HUSH. And the sea stretched out like a pet before its master.

HUSH. And the elements grew calm. HUSH.

The Lord can speak peace to our souls. He says to us "Hush, do not be disturbed. Do not be troubled. It is I—be not afraid. I will not let you fall. I will not let you go down. I will not let your enemy overtake you. I will not let trouble conquer you. I will not let sickness defeat you. I will not let enemies bring you into the dust. I will not let death defeat you. HUSH. HUSH, my child." Be still my soul. The Lord is on your side. Be still when the great storm clouds gather. Be still.

You got the formula. One, keep the Lord on board. Two, do not mind calling him. And three, wait for him to answer. He may not be on your schedule, but he will not arrive late. He never fails. That is the one word that is not in his vocabulary. He will bless your life.

FAITH: WHAT IT IS AND WHAT IT DOES
J. Alfred Smith, Sr.

*In this sermon, we are provided a clear definition of faith
to instruct us that we can overcome faithlessness and
anarchy by heeding God's call to be believers in his
presence, promises, and son, Jesus Christ.*

HEBREWS 11:1–2

WILLIAM BUTLER YEATS uses a poetic paintbrush to describe the unbelief of our time. He wrote: "Things fall apart; the centre cannot hold. Mere anarchy is loosed upon the world . . . The best lack all conviction, while the worst are full of passionate intensity." Our time believes in nothing. Nothing is sacred. Nothing is honorable. It is so because we cannot agree anymore as to what is sacred and honorable. We cannot agree anymore if abortion is right or wrong, if killing is wrong. Murder is not murder. It is either first-degree, second-degree, or accidental murder or homicide. If a soldier kills one in his or her army, it is "friendly fire." Definitions are not clear and specific. A rich medical student from a prestigious family can serve no jail time for allegedly raping a young woman who admits that she came to a man's bedroom after hours. A rich uneducated boxer from a dishonorable background goes to prison when a young lady of her own free will and accord meets the boxer in his bedroom. She screams rape hours after the alleged incident. And the boxer's career is destroyed. The young doctor's career is just beginning. The richer you are the less you pay for insurance. The poorer you are, the higher are your insurance rates. If you ride a boat from Cuba, you are welcome to come to the United States and embrace democracy. If you ride a boat from Haiti in search of democracy, you are not welcome in the United States.

Yeats is correct. Things have fallen apart; the center has not held. Mere anarchy is loosed upon the world.

An Unbelieving World

In this present world moral values are turned upside down. Wrong is right. Right is wrong. Elders are not respected for wisdom, and youth are respected for their cosmetic beauty, so the elders try to be young. There is no respect for authority. Children born yesterday question authority. People with no experience reject those with experience. Profanity is acceptable in public speech and dress. Good manners do not earn respect. Nonviolence is called weakness. Violence is a symbol of strength. Respect is not commanded by character but demanded by threat and intimidation. People want religion without ethics; worship is not for the honoring of God but for religious entertainment. The church calls not for discipleship but for membership.

The Bible was first called the Word of God. Scholars then decided that the Bible *contained* the Word of God. Now the Bible is thought of by the university as another book of literature filled with prescientific myths. They are prescientific because in the Bible nonscientific fairy tales appear, such as Jonah surviving being swallowed by a big fish. Prophet Elijah makes an iron ax head float on water and three young Hebrew men survive the ordeal of a burning, fiery furnace and Jesus turns water to wine and arises the third day from the grave. Who can believe these ancient tales that fail to happen in the modern world?

The world has passed through three historical cycles. First of all, there was the era of faith from A.D. 3 to 1453. Here God was everything and humanity was nothing. Secondly, there was the era of the Renaissance and the Enlightenment. During the Renaissance from 1453 to 1690, humanity and the natural sciences were everything, and God was nothing. During the Enlightenment from 1690 to 1781, humanity and philosophy were everything and God was nothing. Followed by humanity and sociology and psychology being everything in the nineteenth century and God being nothing. Now in the twentieth century, we have moved into the modern era where God is nothing and humanity is nothing. Truly everything seems to be falling apart. Nothing is sacred. Everything is open for criticism and rejection. Power and not morality constitutes authority. The only true god seems to be money. We respect people with the most money, not those with the character of India's Mother Teresa and South Africa's president Nelson Mandela.

God is calling us away from unbelief to faith. Our text reminds us that by faith persons of ancient time won God's approval.

Faith: What It Is?

Reason says, "Seeing is believing." Faith says, "Believing is seeing." Reason says, "I must see cold facts and naked evidence." Faith says, "I would rather walk with God in the darkness of faith than to walk alone in the sunlight of human reason."

God is eternal. Human reason is temporal. Human knowledge is incomplete, temporal, transitory, ever-changing. The human mind, as creative as it is, as imaginative and logical as it is, is limited in experience, limited in knowledge, limited in thinking capacity, and limited in its capacity to remember. The most brilliant mathematical genius has a sharp mind that becomes like a dull knife as age withers the body. But God's matchless memory is from everlasting to everlasting. No one proverb is more appropriate than Proverbs 3:5, which says, "Trust in the Lord with all thine heart, and lean not to thine own understanding" (King James Version).

What is faith? Is it not a leap in the dark? It is not throwing the dice and hoping that your lucky number will appear. It is not a gamble that your lucky lottery number will make you a millionaire overnight. Faith is not a superstitious rabbit's foot or a lucky horseshoe. Faith is not a blind illusion or a stubborn rejection of the facts. Faith is not faith in faith. Faith is not trust in my intellect. It is not trust in my ability to outwit my enemy. It is not confidence in the ability of friends to not let me down. Faith is the ability *to trust completely the presence, power, and promises of God*.

God's presence, power, and promises are unseen realities. I do not deny them because I cannot see them. I do not deny electric currents, yet I do not see them. I do not see soundwaves, yet I use my telephone. I do not see the unseen process which brings a live television program to me, but I enjoy the television program. Why then is it so difficult *to trust completely* the presence, power, and promises of God?

> When we cannot see our way,
> Let us trust and still obey . . .
> J. C. MACAULAY

Faith is being sure that the God we cannot see is nonetheless present. This unseen God is present in power. This unseen God is present with power to keep each promise that He has made to us. What will faith do for us and with us?

Faith: What Does It Do?

Faith transports us into God's presence. Hebrews 11:6 says: "No man can please God without faith. For whoever comes to God must have faith that God exists, and rewards those who seek him" (Good News Bible). How can you doubt God? Psalm 14:1 says: "The fool has said in his heart, there is no God" (KJV). How can you doubt God? There can never be a creature and creation without a creator. There can never be a book without an author. There can never be a building without an architect and builder. Water weighs eight hundred times more than air, yet to have rain, it must be lifted against the force of gravity, held in suspension above the earth, moved to definite locations, and brought down in little drops of rain so no one is drowned. Only God can do that.

Scientists tell us that one little bee is not supposed to fly because the wings of the bee are too small. But God defied the laws of science and enabled the bee's small, weak wings to beat 190 times a second, or 11,400 times a minute. A little bee is a mystery to science. Scholars can explain how one little bee must visit 56,000 clover heads to get nectar for honey. A red clover blossom contains less than an eighth of a grain of sugar. Seven thousand grains are required to make a pound of honey. That one little bee whose wings are too small for it to fly, whose wings are also too weak for it to fly according to science, it obeys God and flies 56,000 times back and forth to her hive, bringing enough clover to make one pound of sugar. Science cannot explain everything. Therefore, science is limited. My faith is in the God who is above science. What does faith do? Faith transports us into God's presence.

Faith moves me to confess in God's presence my inability to save myself by reason or intellect or human knowledge. Faith motivates me to confess that Jesus is my savior. Jesus says in John 14:6, "I am the way, the truth, and the life. No man comes to the Father but by me" (KJV). Salvation is by faith in Jesus Christ. As a man, Jesus got hungry. As God He fed thousands with a boy's lunch. As a man he was lonely; as God, He said, "The Father has not left me alone." As a man he got tired; as God, He said, "Come unto me, all ye that labor and are heavy laden, and I will give you rest."

There has never been anyone like Jesus before Jesus. There has never been anyone like Jesus since Jesus. There never will be another like Jesus. Jesus is the same yesterday, today, and tomorrow.

Faith brings us into God's presence where we confess Jesus. Faith sends us away from God's presence to profess Jesus before an unbelieving world. If a Roman soldier who witnessed the crucifixion of Jesus can profess, "Surely this man must be the Son of God," why can't we profess Jesus as God's son, our savior, to a faithless generation? Jesus, I profess you as my bridge over troubled waters. You are the mountain that overshadows every valley. You are a clear river of fresh water in a hot desert of unbelief.

Faith brings us to God's presence for confession, and away from God's presence for profession. Faith takes us past profession to performance. What is our performance? Our performance is that of service. Profession with our lips don't go far enough. Our hands and feet and our hearts are to perform for the glory and honor of God. Faith is not words about God. Faith works for God.

When doubt says "You can't," faith says "Trust God and get the job done. God put you on earth to get the job done in spite of your handicaps. Faith is the substance of things hoped for, the evidence of things not seen." When logic says it has never been done before, faith answers, "There is a first time for everything." Your friends may discourage you. Your family may refuse to help you. Doors may shut in your face. Fatigue may tire your body. Failure may tell you to stop trying. Get up. Get with it, try again, and never give up.

One night, while staying up late to watch a movie, I saw what faith in God can do. It was a movie about a God-fearing soldier who read his Bible and prayed to God for faith. His name was Lieutenant Clarence E. Coggins. During the Second World War Lieutenant Coggins and his troops were trapped in a foxhole by the Germans. Lieutenant Coggins slipped behind the enemy lines and convinced the German commander that they were surrounded by American troops. This one lone American farmer boy soldier captured 946 Germans and 17 officers. This true story tells us that with strong faith in God you can do the impossible.

When Glenn Cunningham was seven years old, he was so badly burned in a schoolhouse fire in Kansas that there were no toes on his left foot. His right leg became crooked and short by two and one half inches. The doctors said that he would never walk again. He massaged his legs, and the family pulled them, although it caused him great pain. He soon walked with crutches. At the age of eleven he threw his crutches down. He developed his legs. His junior year in high school he made the track team.

In 1934 at Princeton's Palmer Stadium, representing the University of Kansas, he beat Bill Bronthrow of Princeton by forty yards and established the world's indoor mile record.

Conclusion

Only believe. All things are possible, if you only believe. Do you believe? If you have faith, God has the power. . . .

Believe in God's presence.
Believe in God's promises.
Believe in God's power to help you perform.

TEMPT GOD
Howard Thurman

This intensely thought-provoking sermon challenges us to consider our relationship to God by examining Jesus' dilemma in responding to one of the Devil's temptations and taunts. We are instructed that we, as Jesus did, must understand faith in the context of an orderly world which requires our respect for all God's creations.
MATTHEW 4:4–7; LUKE 4:9–12

Temptations of Jesus

We are continuing our thinking together about certain of the dilemmas of Jesus, and today we consider *another* aspect of the dilemma in the wilderness. First, I want to read from the same British poet from whom I read last week.

THE RICH YOUNG RULER
'What must I do, master, to gain
Eternal life?
From my youth I have kept the Commandments,
Honoured my parents;
Theft, murder, lying, adultery —
All these
By God's mercy have passed me by.
What then must I do, master?
What more must I do?
'Sell all,' he replied, 'And follow me.'
An easy saying.
He, a carpenter, a carpenter's son,
Sacrificed nothing.
And his man Peter — smirking, self-righteous —
What did he lose
But some worn nets, a boat-share,
And trade in the market?
It wasn't myself I was thinking of —
Ease and possessions —
But the responsibility of wealth
Towards its dependents.
What of them, if I had obeyed him —
What of my servants?
That's what I tell myself, now —
But do I believe it?
Then — silent — I walked away,

Watching my sandals,
While his voice, the voice of my heart,
Followed me homeward.
In misery, I stopped by the lake.
Hid by the crowd-wall,
I heard him speak of the Kingdom of God,
The camel, the needle.[6]

And then these few sentences by James Lane Allen in *The Choir Invisible:*

"To see justice go down and not believe in the triumph of injustice; for every wrong that you weakly deal another or another deals you to love more and more the fairness and beauty of what is right; and so to turn with ever-increasing love from the imperfection that is in us all to the Perfection that is above us all—the perfection that is God."

The Tempter took him to the pinnacle of the Temple and he said to him,

"If you are the Son of God, jump down from the pinnacle and it will be all right. Nothing will happen to you. Why? Because you are someone very special and God will give his angels charge concerning you, as the Psalmist says, and upon their wings they will beat your feet lest you hurt yourself in some way."

And the Master replied,

"Man must not tempt God, even a good man."

What is the essence of the dilemma? You have thought of it many times and it is all so familiar that anything I say to you this morning you may have heard before, but nevertheless I am going to say it.

The Tempter said to him that this world is not orderly. It is not structured. There is no fundamental dependability upon which the individual living expression of life may depend. But if you can manage to get into a certain position of immunity, then the ordinary logic of life can be handled and manipulated.

The implication of the Master's reply to the Tempter is this:

If I go up to the pinnacle of the Temple and jump down, the possibilities are I will break my neck, Son of God to the contrary notwithstanding, because this is an orderly world and if I act as though I am immune to the logic, the logic itself will destroy me.

Do you believe that?

Life is rooted and grounded in a structure of dependability. It is this that makes it possible for the private enterprise, or the collective enterprise, to be sustained by life. If I ignore this fact, then the very force of life itself becomes an instrument of death in my hands. Let's see what this means in terms of the intimate dilemma which Jesus faced.

We experience it in our own time. The mind of man has been activating its affinity with the external world of nature, and as a result, man has been able to lift out of the world of nature many things which are inherent in its order. As man has lifted these things out and observed them and reduced them to manageable units of control and manipulation, he has made the order of nature become an instrument in his hands for the fulfillment of private ends, ends which themselves may be destructive of the very nature that gave the secret in the first place. And that means, in simple terms, that when the secret of atomic energy becomes available to man and man uses this knowledge, skill, power, and insight for ends that are exclusive of his fellows — in other words, when he uses it in ways that will give him a kind of immunity against the moral quality of human relations — then the very order itself, the very logic itself, the very energy of the atom itself becomes the stalking manifestation of the *wrath* of God. But if he uses the knowledge for ends that are inclusive of his fellows and their needs, the very energy itself becomes a manifestation of the *love* of God. When man experiences that kind of community, achievements of health and meaning and vitality and fulfillment become available unlike anything that has harassed or haunted his mind through all the generations of the past.

One other word in this connection. There is something even more personal here, it seems to me. It is reasonable for a man to say: If I am good, if I try to do the best I can, if I have followed the law of my heart, and in ways that were deliberate and conscious, tried to understand the will of God and put myself at its disposal, if I have not withheld my compassion from the needy, and have offered my thanksgiving to God for all of the manifestations of graces by which he has surrounded and sustained my life, if I have an inner sense of harmony and peace with His Spirit—then this ought to give me certain pragmatic advantages in life. I ought to be privileged to be an exception to the rules that bind people who have not been acting this way. Have you ever felt that way? Consider something you yourself are experiencing, and then look across the street and see a person who, from your point of view, has violated everything that you regard as holy and sacred. Yet— what he touches seems to blossom, and what you touch seems to wither and die as soon as it looks in your face. It's peculiar. You have felt that way!

Jesus may have thought:

Somehow the quality of my character ought to render me immune to the order of life. Life should make an exception in my case because I am Jesus! Because of that great moment when I felt the affirmation and the confirmation of my Father! When he gave to me the complete and utter sanction and imprimatur of His whole Being, under the aegis and sweep of that sense of glory and communion and identity, I seemed to have been lifted out of all the categories by which men are bound and held. Why can't I, then, act with utter disregard for all of this?

A friend of mine, who is a doctor, was the dean of a medical school once upon a time. Many years ago I went to him for a physical examination. I was making a change in my plan of life and I wanted to know what was working for me and what would be working against me. He gave me his part of the exam and then sent me to about five other people to do various things. At the end of about a week I got a telephone call from him telling me that he wanted to see me. You know the sense of destiny that rides on that. You walk into his office; you sit in the chair and he sits at his desk. He has a manila folder and in it there are sheets of paper with typing and graphs and a lot of things you don't understand. He opens the folder, looks at you, and says, "Hmmm, hmmmm . . . Uhmmm." Then he hesitates on one page, looks at you again, and then, it is a great relief, he turns it over and says, "Hmmm." And so he goes, all the way through. Well, that's what my doctor did, and I rejoiced to see him close the folder. I knew that I had made it. Then he said to me, "You are in fine shape. Your heart, your lungs, all those things are in good order, but you are too heavy."

He talked with me rather learnedly about what the extra pounds I was carrying would do to my heart and lungs and blood vessels — all kinds of things that were very frightening to me. Then I looked at him! He wasn't as tall as I, and he weighed about 225 pounds. *He thought that his body knew that he was a doctor.* His body did not know that he was a doctor; his body knew precisely what my body knew. We were bound by the same relentless logic of orderedness that provides the structure of dependability for life. Because he knew something about the structure had no bearing on this fact. It gave him no immunity, unless his knowledge enabled him to operate more fully, more effectively, more creatively *within* the order than my lack of knowledge.

This is a part of the dilemma of the trained mind, isn't it? Because we are trained, because we know so much about some things, in very subtle ways this counsels us into a kind of delusion about the extent to which we ourselves are just a part of the ebb and flow and order of life. Unless the knowledge gives us insight that will enable us to function in ways that will use the structure of dependability as a resource for the highest fulfillment in life, then the very knowledge that we have tempts us to put ourselves against life. And very quietly, without blasting of trumpets, without making any noise, life just grinds us to powder.

This is what the Master saw:

With all the embodiment which I feel of the very living Spirit of God, with all the "for instances" of His Kingdom, and the Angelos of His Spirit that has as its fundamental purpose the renewing and the regenerating of life so that more and more, all of life will come under the sweep of the gentle approval of the Will and Mind of the Love of God; nevertheless, I still must operate within the structure that *holds*. When I get out of it, life becomes the Enemy. When I am in it, life becomes the Resource. When I get out of it I experience the Wrath of God. When I am within it I experience the Love of God.

And the Tempter carried him to the pinnacle of the Temple and said:

It is all right for you to jump. God will guarantee you.

If the dilemma were real, if the temptation were real, Jesus could have failed. If he could not have failed, there is no meaning in his freedom. I am so very glad that he struggled and triumphed. And so he speaks to me all the time that I might struggle, if, happily, I too might triumph. But if I felt that when the pressure was upon him, he had an out, then when the pressure is upon me I could not hear him, speak to me. Because he triumphed, there is laid upon my soul a necessity that I can never shake, that there is a way. There is a way.

Leave us not, our Father, to the strength of our weakness or the weakness of our strength. Hold us, O God, hold us until at last there begins to move deep within us the response to Thy Love. This is what we want, O God, so much, so very, very much, our Father.

TALKING TO A DEAD MAN
A. Safiyah Fosua

Using Adam Clayton Powell and Lazarus as metaphors, this sermon informs us that we are dead before we are resurrected by our acceptance of Christ. Jesus, through his resurrection of Lazarus and Powell, brought many followers to him and gave them, the living dead, new life.
JOHN 12:9–11; EPHESIANS 2:1

I̶N *ADAM BY Adam: The Autobiography of Adam Clayton Powell, Jr.,* Adam Clayton Powell pens these words:

> "On Good Friday night, 1930, I preached my trial sermon. It was a strange crowd that listened—all the girls from the Cotton Club, others from the downtown night clubs, girls of every color, bootleggers, gamblers, all the fantastic array of acquaintances I had accumulated through the years. I can still remember the sight. They all came to laugh. 'Adam's going to preach!' Adam, who played one of the best games of stud poker, who had bet every cent he had in his pocket on one roll of dice, who had slept with more women than anyone could count, and who could hold more liquor than anybody in his circle, was going to be a preacher! . . . Thirty-seven people joined the church that night."[7]

Why did thirty-seven people join the church that night? They joined because of the surprising change in Adam Clayton Powell, Jr. They were accustomed to a man who was dead in trespasses and sins. That night, they saw a new Adam. Jesus called Adam Clayton Powell, Jr., back from the dead, just as he had called Lazarus out of the grave and back from the dead. The old Adam was dead but the new Adam was resurrected in Christ.

Lazarus was a well-known man in Bethany. He was probably a wealthy man. He had two sisters whom we mention often in song, Mary and Martha. Mary, Martha, and Lazarus were close friends of Jesus'. If you remember the story of the raising of Lazarus from the dead, you will recall the personal notice that Jesus received of Lazarus' threatened health. In Scripture, we saw Jesus purposely waiting where he was until Lazarus was dead, in order to draw attention to the power of God.

The disciples didn't even understand what Jesus was doing. They only understood that it was dangerous for Jesus to go to Bethany, which was only a couple of miles from Jerusalem, with the political scene so hot. The religious leaders, who wanted to kill Jesus for the "good of the country," were looking for any excuse. They thought that Jesus was being cautious about his life.

I hope when you read this passage, you see real people. So often we read the Bible as though everyone mentioned was a superhero and a super-Christian. Though they were notable people—we call them heroes and sheroes—they were still people. They were also people of color. Mary and Martha might have been like some sisters that we know. They were fairly well-off. If they had been around today, they might have bought them some nails and some hair. Are you getting a visual yet? As well-to-do people, they no doubt provided financial backing for Jesus' ministry. Seen in this context, the issue becomes more serious.

"We sent money and you mean to tell me that he couldn't *make* time?"

"This man has had his feet under my dinner table and he let my brother die? I don't know if I can even talk to him for a while."

What was it like when Mary saw him from a distance? I wonder if that sister rolled her eyes? Or did she say to her friends: "Look, here he comes now, a day late and a dollar short!" I suspect that she had something to say about Jesus' absence. Scripture only records a portion of her complaint.

> "Lord, if you had been here . . ." I'm sure that there was more.
> "Lord, you could have done something about this. . . . Where were you?"
> "Lord, I needed you and you were not here!"

Isn't that the way our lives are sometimes? We need God—right now! Not tomorrow, not in three days. Right now! If, however, I am reading this story correctly, it seems that there will be some days when hope must seem to die so that the power of God can be realized more fully. There were several things that Jesus could *not* have done if he had merely prevented Lazarus' death.

Jesus used the miracle of Lazarus' resurrection to challenge local ideas about death and resurrection. Sadducees believed that there was no resurrection. Jewish folk theology, probably Pharisee, felt that the spirit hovered around the dead body for three days looking for an opportunity to reenter. They felt that after the third day, there was no return, for the spirit had gone on to the afterlife. This particular resurrection, though the third recorded in Jesus' ministry, took place on the fourth day in the grave. Lazarus was definitely dead and gone — as a matter of fact, he was stinking dead! Jesus must be the resurrection and the life!

It becomes very important at this point to highlight the significance of resurrection. The facts pertaining to the death, burial, and resurrection of Christ are more than just a cliché to tack onto the end of an otherwise meaningless sermon. The implications of the death, burial, and resurrection of Christ are for each believer, both in this life and in that which is to come. The whole idea of salvation is that of being saved from death.

Some years ago, I heard about a Canadian evangelist who traveled along the countryside with a coffin. He carried a sign that said: "Come Tonight and SEE a Dead Man." The people would flock out to the revival tent to see what was in the casket. At an appropriate time, he would open the coffin and the people would file by. Inside the coffin was a mirror. The people were dead, so the story goes, and didn't know it.

Salvation comes when we recognize that each of us is dead in trespasses and sins before we accept Christ (Ephesians 2:1). There is a living death on this side of the grave, which consists of not being in fellowship with God. And there is another death on the other side of the grave which consists of eternal separation from God. Baptism dramatizes this reality. We are buried, yet snatched out of the grave because of the work of Jesus Christ in our personal life!

Our fathers and mothers understood this concept of being dead before Jesus comes into our lives. Someone, back in the 1930s, had the insight to send interviewers to record the testimonies of a number of older African Americans who had been released from slavery. It was believed that in order to be born again, the old person had to die first.

The narratives share a common thread. The believer often fell into a state of trance or had a dream. There they would see themselves either dying or bound for hell. In the background they would often hear a voice, maybe their own voice, crying out to God for mercy. Then came the rescue . . . the angel of the Lord or even Jesus himself would rescue them from the reality of a burning hell.

When they came to themselves,
they'd look at their hands, and their hands looked new
they'd look at their feet and they would too!
The places they used to go
The things they used to do . . .

Though much time has gone by, much of the same imagery can be applied to some of our conversion experiences. In modern times, A.M.E. Bishop John Bryant of Texas and Sierra Leone tells of a dream at the age of ten where Satan chased him to kill him. . . . Jesus stepped in and said: "Choose me and live, or take your chances with him."[8] Rev. Joseph Black of Cleveland tells of being spared from a gambling raid by a voice that told him to cash in his chips and leave. The next day in church, that same voice of God spoke to him to "Confess or die!"[9] Rev. Preston Washington, a prominent Baptist pastor in Harlem, tells of how the Lord touched his life when he was dying of malaria in Nigeria. After his transformation he began to serve God in seriousness. . . .[10] In spite of all of our modern sophistication, God still chooses to reveal himself to many of us in ancient ways.

The apostle Paul says it a different way:

I am crucified, or put to death with Christ, yet I live. You
    see, the irony is,
that I don't have my old life any more. The life that I now
    live, I live by
the faith of the son of God who loved me and gave himself
    for me.

(GALATIANS 2:20)

In Paul's letter to the Romans we are reminded that we are buried with Christ in baptism and that we rise in Christ to walk in the newness of life.

An old baptismal practice in the Middle East involves picking up a rock from the riverbed while being immersed. Once on the shore, the newly baptized would throw the rock back to the spot where they were baptized and say: "That's where I died!" Perhaps it is time for some of us to return to that place where we threw our rock. To look back at where we died to trespasses and sins and became alive in Christ. We can never allow ourselves to lose sight of the reality that we were just as dead as Lazarus before Jesus called each one of our names.

Have you ever thought about the kind of testimony that Lazarus must have had when he was raised? Something about testimony in the life of the African-American church has fueled the fires of revival and kept us focused when we were discouraged. When we could not read the Bible, the oral tradition of "telling the story" carried us through. When we did not know all the supposedly "theologically correct" things to say, we simply told the story as we knew it in our hearts. Scholars, who wanted to understand the factors that influence conversion, have done a number of expensive studies. They were surprised to find that personal testimony often carried more weight than hearing scriptural canon. Being able to hear and to see the evidence of a God who is real, yet alive, and not impotent, carries more weight for the unbeliever than mere "holy words on a page." The written tradition is important to strengthen and deepen our faith, but most of us come to faith by *hearing the story* and by seeing results.

We are losing, in some churches, the ability to sell our story. At one time you could not stop us from telling our story; now only a few of the brave are willing to tell of the activity of God in their own individual lives. When we realized that we were oppressed, we could tell of victories of faith. When we were aware of the day-to-day struggle, simply surviving and being alive to testify were victories in themselves. Now that we have houses that we didn't build, and land that we didn't plant ourselves . . . to echo the words of Deuteronomy, we have done the same things that Israel did. We have forgotten, far too quickly, that we are still in bondage, and that even getting to where we are did not happen by our own personal strength. All that we have comes from the Lord.

Well Lazarus told his story. He must have set the house on fire because John 12:9 and 10 tell us that the crowds were just not coming to see Jesus but also to see Lazarus. So, the chief priests made plans to kill Lazarus as well, because his testimony was causing many to come to faith.

Conclusion

As we return to the opening testimony of Adam Clayton Powell, we find that people gathered in great number to hear a man who had been dead. They found a man brought back to life by the power of the resurrection of Christ. As a result they were saved. The early slaves spoke of their conversion as though they had died and come back to life again.

Lazarus in this morning's text had been raised from the dead and had now become, because of his testimony, as much a threat to the Devil as Jesus was. *That's why they wanted to kill him as much as they wanted to kill Jesus!*

You know what? The religious leaders didn't think far enough ahead. They were correct in understanding that one must kill a leader in order to kill a movement. They were also correct in their understanding that Lazarus' tremendous testimony was just as convincing as being with Jesus himself. Yet, they forgot about the rest of the people scattered throughout the countryside with tremendous testimonies of the power of God!

You see, if the religious leaders killed Jesus, and Lazarus, there were still other witnesses in a growing cast of thousands that included the *man born blind* who could say:

He opened my dead eyes!

There was an old sick man, who had been laying by the pool for years waiting on a miracle. He had been sick for so long that he began to grumble and complain all the time.

Do you know anybody like that?

You almost have to wonder if he had learned to prefer sickness to health.

One day Jesus came into his life

Get up from there
You don't have to lay there anymore
Pick up your bed and walk!
I can imagine that he walked through the city, testifying about
his old condition. I can see him testifying about the *dysfunction* that
goes along with being sick for so long. But "Here I stand by the
grace of God!"

There were a number of *lepers,*
with flesh rotting off their bodies
stinking like dead men
literally walking dead.
One day Jesus restored their flesh.
Suddenly they were not the walking dead anymore.
Suddenly people were not afraid of them anymore.
He sent them home to live with their families again.

Can you hear their testimonies? I was an outcast. I was a
stinker. I was a zombie because of the way the drugs had wiped
me out! I couldn't come home because my wife was afraid of me. I
couldn't be around people because they were afraid of me. But one
day, Jesus came into my life and made me whole!

Then there was a woman, you know her, with an issue of blood.
She couldn't seem to get cured.
She tried the doctors at the hospital.
She tried the herbalist.
She called a psychic.
And still she couldn't get any better.
One day, She determined in her heart to *try Jesus!*
I can see her crawling down around people's feet holding
her clothes close to her so nobody would notice the smell
trying to cover up her face so that people wouldn't run from her
(She was unclean, you know!)
Scooting in between their feet
Crawling around on the ground
Thinking, "If I could just touch the hem of his garment!"
When the encounter was all over, you couldn't shut her up.
He's a doctor in a sickroom!
He's a waymaker!

He's a lawyer in the courtroom!
He healed my body and told me to run on!
If you can't tell it, let me tell it!
If you can't thank him, let me thank him!
Said I wasn't gonna tell nobody—but I couldn't keep it to myself!

No, the religious leaders did not think far enough ahead. Stopping Lazarus would not be enough to stop the church. They seem to have forgotten that there were men who were once blind but were now able to see. They were running through the countryside—telling their stories. If, by some chance, they might have been able to find them and silence them, there was at least one Gadarene demoniac testifying that he was finally able to come home. The Pharisees and the chief priests should have considered all of these people dangerous. There were the lepers, and that noisy woman with the issue of blood—all telling their stories!

And then, there you are. . . .

Did you know that your story is dangerous?

You are a dangerous used-to-be-deaf person who has been healed to hear God's voice!

You are a dangerous used-to-be-lame person, leaping and dancing and praising the lord!

You are the demoniac that used to be out of your mind, now able to go home without shame!

You are the person with a right to sing

Amazing grace
How sweet the sound
that saved a wretch
like me
I once was lost
But now I am found
was blind but now I see!

Stand up and take your place with Lazarus! No one can silence your story!

MOVING FROM ENDANGERMENT TO EMPOWERMENT
Raymond Lee Harris, Jr.

This sermon informs us how the church can help African Americans to view themselves as empowered people as opposed to oppressed members of society. We do this by believing in God, making a commitment to God's mission, and receiving the power of the Lord.
JOHN 20:19–22

A CRISIS EXISTS among our males—particularly the younger generation. My brothers, we occupy a precarious position in this country. The reasons as to why we find ourselves in such a critical situation can be summarized in two arresting sentences that I read in a theme paper on this very subject: "There is an increasing disintegration in the quality and structure of African-American families evidenced by the systematic degradation of the African-American male. . . . From birth to death, African-American males have a short and dangerous path."[11]

The theme paper continues by describing at least five contributing factors that lead to the degradation of our men. I would like to touch upon them briefly before we move on to our text from the Sacred Scriptures.

First of all, the author writes that there is a lack of *male* role models in the classroom, in the church, and in the home. Notice that in making this statement I did *not* say that women cannot serve as role models. They can; but the problem is that there seems to be a lack of *male* role models in these three important areas in the life of a young person. For instance, it has been conjectured that the reason why it is difficult for some young African-American males to think about whether God is calling them to the priesthood is due to the fact that they have little interaction with African-American priests.

Another factor is the overly negative portrayal of our men in society. We are presumed dangerous until it is proven otherwise. On top of that, high rates of unemployment and underemployment among us has affected our mental health and our marriages. Even if some of us seem to be advancing up the career ladder, we discover later that there is a "glass ceiling" in which we can go no farther, while our European-American counterparts of equal or even less skill pass us by.

The third factor contributing to the degradation of African-American males is the "failure of the educational system to motivate and retain students."[12] We find that in Baltimore City, the dropout rate for African-American students, whether male or female, is about 55 percent. This happens, in part, because some teachers, parents or guardians, and the students themselves have low expectations regarding their ability to excel in education. Even in those situations in which the teachers and administrators are working hard to produce a quality education for our children, we find that they are hampered by a lack of financial resources to buy the tools necessary to bring such a desired result to fruition.

The final factor is the existence of high rates of crime and violence in our communities. There is nothing sadder than to read the morning newspaper or to watch the late news on television report the latest wave of violence in our city. This phenomenon has been fueled by the proliferation of the drug trade, which is just an example of the existence in all sectors of our society of a relentless pursuit of financial and material gain by any means necessary — even at the expense of human life. If we look at the statistics, we find that the leading cause of death among African-American males aged fifteen to twenty-four is homicide. While we constitute only 6 percent of the general population, we constitute over 45 percent of the prison population in this country.

When we consider these four factors, we know that there is something seriously wrong in this country and that the Church — the People of God — must respond and act.

❦The Church must respond in a prophetic manner and ask questions of the government as to why we can have conferences to help other countries in this world and cannot figure out how to help the urban areas of this nation.

❦The Church must respond in a prophetic manner and ask why there is a disparity between how urban and suburban children are educated in the state of Maryland.

❦The Church must respond in a prophetic manner and provide a model to society in regards to the fostering of healthy and supportive relationships.

❦The Church must respond in a prophetic manner and use occasions such as this day to celebrate the presence in this country of millions of African-American males who are:

engaged in loving and committed marriages, having successful careers, serving as positive role models for our children,
developing their academic skills as well as their athletic
skills, able to make their stumbling blocks into stepping-
stones to a better life, and living lives committed to the Lord.

❦ And finally, the Church must respond to this crisis in a
prophetic manner by reminding our men who they really are
and *to whom* they belong so that they can maintain or regain
confidence in themselves.

One of the ways in which the Church can do this is through the
proclamation and the preaching of the Word of God. For it is in the
Word of God that we find divine instructions for daily living. As I
read this theme paper and read the Gospel appointed for this Sunday, I asked the Lord for a word to give to His people. What must
the men in this parish do to take their rightful place in our Church,
in our families, and in our society? How, O Lord, are we going to
move from talking about ourselves as being endangered members
of society into seeing ourselves as empowered men of God?

As I continued to meditate on this passage of Scripture, I found
that the Lord has a message for us; and the message is this: If
African-American males are going to move from endangerment to
empowerment, then we must believe that the Risen Lord has appointed and anointed us for service.

BELIEVE IN THE RISEN LORD *(John 20:19–20)*

We find in the beginning of our text that on Sunday evening, the
disciples were locked up in a room because they were ashamed
that their leader had been crucified at the hands of the Roman op-
pressors; and they were afraid that they would be next.

Then we read that the Risen Lord—who had appeared to Mary
Magdalene early that morning—suddenly appeared in their midst.
His presence brought his disciples out of fear into feelings of joy
and peace in the knowledge that the Lord was truly risen.

I would submit to you that as we meditate on this passage of scripture, we must renew our belief in the Risen Lord as well; because today some of the disciples of Christ are gathering in churches that seem to be locked up because they are fearful of the outside world. Yes, we may boldly profess our belief in the Risen Lord when we step into the church building, but the moment we step out of the church and into our homes, schools, and places of employment, some of us act as if we are ashamed and afraid of being identified as being Christians.

That is why Christianity is not attractive to the unchurched, because some Christians seem to be timid people who are following a Jesus who is portrayed in the media as "weak and lowly." But that is not the Jesus that I read about in my Bible. Yes, Jesus was a tenderhearted person who was moved with pity when he saw that the crowds who followed him "were troubled and abandoned, like sheep without a shepherd" (Matthew 9:36). However, that does not mean that he was not a strong person. My Jesus was not "weak and lowly" — he was tough.

Jesus was tough in the sense that he was unyielding in his determination to carry out the will of God in his life. In spite of opposition, he remained faithful to the task that was entrusted to him. Jesus was tough.

He was one who taught on his own authority, unlike the scribes and the Pharisees. He cast out demons. He threw the money changers out of the temple. He confronted injustice. Jesus was tough.

When they threatened him with death, he kept on going and stuck to his principles. He tried to preach about the Reign of God, but the forces opposed to its advancement tried to stop that message by nailing him to the cross . . . but early on Sunday morning, our God raised Jesus from the dead; and now all of his enemies are under his feet because he "holds the keys to death and the nether world" (Revelation 1:18). Jesus was tough.

Jesus wants his followers to be tough — to move from being a fearful people to being a faithful people. He wants his followers to go out into our community not ashamed of his gospel, because it is the "power of God for the salvation of everyone who believes"

(Romans 1:16). Before you go out into the community, you must realize that the Risen Lord has appointed you *to serve.*

APPOINTED TO SERVE *(John 20:21)*

That means that if we are going to confess to the world that we are disciples of Jesus Christ, then we must make a commitment to continue his saving and liberating mission in our communities. We have been appointed to serve for the glory of God and for the good of humanity, not for the self-gratification of our egos.

Therefore, my brothers, when you take your rightful place in the family—if you are married, then you create a relationship with your wife that is not based on subservience but rather on mutual respect and mutual submission to each other and to the Lord. It means that you make your marriage the sacrament that it is supposed to be and tell your children: "As for me and my house, we are going to serve the Lord" (Joshua 24:15).

When you take your rightful place in the society—that means that you use the gifts, talents, and blessings that God has given to you to bless someone else. You go into a society that views you negatively and you say: "I don't care what society says about me; I know what the Scriptures say—that I am created in the image of God and that everything that God created is good."

When you take your rightful place in the Church—that means that you don't come in here thinking that you are going to amass your own power and build your own little kingdom; because what you do for Christ is for his greater glory and for the building up of his kingdom.

We have been appointed to serve. However, we cannot fulfill our appointment to serve without being anointed by the Spirit of the living God.

ANOINTED TO SERVE *(John 20:22)*

I know that if we go further into this chapter, we find the scriptural reference for our Catholic belief in the Sacrament of

Penance. But the reason why I stopped at the twenty-second verse for the purposes of this homily is because it reminded me of another saying of Jesus that we find in the Acts of the Apostles.

> But you will receive power when the Holy Spirit comes upon you. And you will be my witnesses . . . to the ends of the earth (Acts 1:8).

The Church did not publicly profess its belief in the Risen Lord and put it into practice until it was empowered by the Spirit at Pentecost. So it is with us. We cannot fulfill our mission by our own power. It has to come from the power of God.

We received that power when we celebrated the Sacrament of Confirmation. When we were confirmed, the bishop or the priest anointed our foreheads with oil—as a tangible sign of the descent of the Holy Spirit upon us—and prayed, "Be sealed with the gift of the Holy Spirit." In that prayer, we asked God to give us the fullness of the Holy Spirit that we received at our baptisms. Now, my brothers and sisters, there is no question that God did His part and breathed His spirit upon us. But the question remains, Did we receive it? My brothers, have you stirred into flame the gift of the Holy Spirit that has been given to you? As I remarked in the beginning of this homily, African-American males are in a precarious position in this society. As we continue through life and face the negative things that come our way, we cannot persevere by relying on our own power. We have to rely on the power of God.

I know that the reason why I am able to stand here this afternoon is a result of the power of God in my life. As I ask myself the questions . . .

🌿What was it that enabled me to go on after my father's death in 1984?

🌿What was it that enabled me to get a degree from Princeton University when the odds were against me to graduate?

🌿What was it that enabled me to endure the lonely and depressing times?

🌿Why am I standing here a week after my twenty-fifth birthday when I had a one-in-twenty-one chance of being killed by my twenty-fifth birthday?

🌿What is it that enables me to get back up after I have sinned, and turn back to God and continue to strive to be faithful to the Gospel?

When I think about the answer to my question, I realize that I did not do it by my own power. It is nothing but the power of God.

Conclusion

As I bring this message to a conclusion, I challenge the men of this parish to rely on the power of God. Because some people will say that in order for us to move from endangerment to empowerment, we need political power. But political power alone, when it is unchecked, will corrupt.

On the other hand, some will say that we need economic power. But if we rely on that alone, then we will start worshiping the god of materialism rather than the God of our salvation.

But if you let the power of God that dwells within you undergird your life as you move from endangerment to empowerment, then the political candidate that you voted for could lose, or you could lose your job, but because you relied on the power of God in your life, you can say that no matter what happens I still have hope because "this joy that I have [inside of me], the world didn't give it to me and the world cannot take it away."

Yes, my brothers, you need that something inside so strong that enables you to say that: "I know that I can make it! Even though some sectors of society think that I am no good because I am an African-American male, I know that I can make it! 'For my strength and courage is in the Lord, and He has been my savior' (Psalms 118:14). I know I can make it! 'I shall not die, but live, and declare the works of the Lord' " (Psalms 118:17).

STRANGE DELIVERANCE
H. Beecher Hicks, Jr.

God delivers us from our oppressed existence in strange and mysterious ways because He demands our unconditional surrender and that we recognize his power and ongoing work.

EXODUS 8:1–2

IT IS THE nature of God to deliver those who are oppressed. The activity of God, recorded in Sacred Scripture, is persistent in its claim that wherever oppression is God always shows up. It may be in Ezekiel's valley, or down by the banks of the Babylon where slaves refused to sing, in Daniel's den or the burning furnace of three Hebrew boys; the Scriptures tell us that if pain is there, if poverty is there, if oppression is there God always shows up. God is always involved in the work of rescue and redemption. It is so because it is in the nature of God to deliver those who are oppressed.

Faith, standing on the underpinnings of human history, declares that in every age God delivers.

Ask the survivors of Nazi Germany and the ovens of Auschwitz and they will surely tell you that God delivers;

Ask those of us who are the sons and daughters of slavery, the products of the middle passage, and the offspring of the auction block;

Ask those who, on these shores, suffered under the most demonic form of racism known to man;

Ask those whose great-grandmothers were raped and whose great-grandfathers were castrated, and whose great-aunts and great-uncles were hunted down by bloodhounds and hung on lynching trees;

Ask the countless millions languishing under South African apartheid, ask the children of Soweto and Crossroads who looked one day and saw Nelson Mandela emerge from his prison cell spiritually strong, intellectually alert, and mentally keen and even they will tell you that God delivers.

God delivers because it is in the nature of God to deliver those who are oppressed.

So patently clear is the record of God's deliverance that it barely requires argument. That which amazes me is not the *IF* of

God's deliverance but the *HOW* of God's deliverance. By whatever method, by whatever design, God specializes in *STRANGE DELIVERANCE*! In the morning of creation God inaugurated His creative activity EX NIHILO. He made something out of nothing. That's strange. In the pursuit of the God-ness of God, God sort of leans toward the peculiar:

❧ Who else but God builds boats on dry land?

❧ Who else but God sets bushes on fire but will not burn them up?

❧ Who else but God would send the wind to resurrect dry bones and dead bodies in a cemetery of the slain? That's strange.

When it comes to setting captives free God has a strange methodology.

Here, this "strangeness" of God is to be found in the unfolding of Israel's Exodus experience. The children of Israel found themselves in Egypt because of famine in Israel. Joseph, the son of Jacob, was in charge of the department of agriculture. Soon, however, a new pharaoh arose in Egypt "which knew not Joseph." Suddenly the children of Israel found themselves in bitter bondage, required to make brick without straw and mortar without clay. Their lot was hard, their road was long and yet, the Exodus writer declares:

". . . the more they afflicted them, the more
they multiplied and grew . . .
and they made their lives bitter with
hard bondage" (Exodus 1:12,14).

It was, however, in this moment of affliction and in this moment of bitter bondage that God decided to deliver his people. The God who had walked in Eden would now walk in Egypt. In the moment of Israel's greatest difficulty God began to act. The Word says:

"And the Lord said, I have surely seen
the affliction of my people which are in Egypt,
and have heard their cry by reason of their
taskmasters; for I know their sorrows;
And I am come down to DELIVER them out of
the hand of the Egyptians. . . ." (Exodus 3:7–8).

That's what God does. God delivers. God specializes in delivery. God's occupation is to take men from where they are to where He wants them to be. God specializes in fixing futures, and redirecting destinies, and redesigning history. God delivers. In fact, it is in the being of God, it is in the God-ness of God, it is in the nature of God to deliver those who are oppressed.

I am engaged by this notion of STRANGE DELIVERANCE. God sent Moses along with Aaron to stand before Pharaoh and declare the message: *"LET MY PEOPLE GO!"* But if Pharaoh would not let them go, God told Moses to tell Pharaoh, "if you do not let my people go . . .

❦ "I will smite with the rod that is in mine hand upon the waters which are in the river, and they shall be turned to blood.

❦ "I will smite all thy borders with frogs.

❦ "Say unto Aaron, stretch out thy rod, and smite the dust of the land, that it may become lice throughout all the land of Egypt.

❦ "I will send swarms of flies upon thee, and upon thy servants, and upon thy people . . . and the houses of the Egyptians shall be full of swarms of flies. . . ."

"Moses, I'm not playing. Tell Pharaoh to let my people go. But if that won't work tell him,

❦ "If you refuse to let them go . . . behold the hand of the Lord will be on your cattle, in the field, on the horses, on the donkeys, on the camels, on the oxen, and on the sheep—a very severe pestilence.

❧"Take a handful of ash from the furnace and throw it toward the heavens and boils will break out in sores on man and beast throughout all the land of Egypt.

❧"Stretch out your hand toward heaven, that there may be hail in all the land of Egypt. In the midst of the heat, I'll send hail. I'll send thunder on one side and hail on the other.

"And if that doesn't work, Moses, I'll send locusts to cover the face of the earth so that no one will be able to see the earth. And if that doesn't work I'll send darkness. He calls himself Ra, the sun god, the god of light, but I'll turn his lightbulb out and the darkness will be so thick you can feel it. Tell Pharaoh to let my people go!"

But wait! God decided to deliver Israel from Egypt with blood in water, frogs, lice, pestilence, boils, hail, locusts, and darkness. That's all God used. God ought to do better than this. God's got greater devices at his hand than this. It's sort of beneath God to be caught up in frogs and lice and locusts and such. It's hard to understand God's methodology. However you look at it this is STRANGE DELIVERANCE.

There is something about bondage which transcends the boundaries of time. The reality is that bondage is still upon us. It does not require keen insight or probing analysis to understand that bondage is a recurring reality while freedom is an elusive dream.

There is a bondage that has occasioned a disruption of the family and the incapacity of our schools to affect our children either socially, morally, or intellectually.

There is a bondage that has given rise to a reality of violence that has a stranglehold on our cities. Life has no value. The blood that runs in our streets has placed an indelible stain on the souls of a people.

There is a bondage for which we have developed a rather sophisticated language. The watchwords of our generation are "misery index," and "underclass," and "downward social mobility." But what it really means is that there is now afoot in our society a kind of meaninglessness and loneliness and despair that promotes self-destruction, chaos, anarchy, and death.

We must even look to ourselves, for in many instances we have brought upon ourselves the very bondage we deplore and seek to escape. Just look at us: preoccupied with our own pleasure, prime examples of a culture of consumption, living in the tension of private poverty and the pretensions of public opulence. We have forsaken the struggle, we have forgotten where we came from, we have abandoned the dream, we have deserted the faith of our fathers and mothers, we have abandoned the spiritual roots that made us the people we are, we have lost our prayer power and with it the moral authority to lead our people or to guide our children. There is bondage in the land.

There is bondage in the land, I tell you. And here comes the preacher talking about what God can do with frogs, and lice, and pestilence, and boils, and hail, and locusts, and darkness. That's STRANGE DELIVERANCE.

You must never forget that this entire confrontation between Moses and Pharaoh had its genesis in Pharaoh's attempt to kill the male children. God's entry into the "delivery business" was occasioned by Pharaoh's determination that the men had to be destroyed. Pharaoh was concerned that a liberator, a Messiah, would rise up from within the enslaved community and destroy his economic base of free labor, and consequently the male of the species had to be destroyed.

The scene has changed, the nation has changed, the Pharaoh has changed, but the reality remains the same. The system is designed to destroy the male. Congress has passed no law, the President has issued no executive order, the City Council has passed no ordinance, but the reality is that it appears that "a decree has gone out that every African-American male must die."

I need not bore you with the statistical reality, but the record ought to be clear about Pharaoh's activity. The truth of the matter is that:

🦋African-American males have the lowest life expectancy of any group in this country;

🦋African-American males are more likely to die before the age of twenty and least likely to reach the age of sixty than anybody else in this country;

❧African-American males are most likely to be killed before we reach the age of thirty.

❧We are most likely to die from a drug overdose; most likely to commit suicide; and African-American males represent not only the greatest likelihood of physical casualties but are, in fact, the most self-destructive group in this society.

The vast majority of African-American males are locked up in prisons during their most productive years. They have been removed not by physical death but by institutional death. Because of the nature of the world they live in many have internalized violent, self-destructive ideas before they reach the age of ten. But this is not a cause. This is a reaction to the fact that Pharaoh has decreed that the male children should be killed.

There must be some reason, there must be some logical explanation why God uses such a strange methodology. Surely, there must be some rational understanding for how God uses inarticulate, weak, and minuscule matter in order to effect his purposes and his priorities. I need to understand in an ultimate sense how God always seems to use the unexplainable by the means of the unconventional to bring to pass the unpredictable and to achieve the deliverance of his people and the achievement of his will.

At surface level, there is a temptation to suggest that what we have here is God's ability to bring down the strong through the instruments of the weak. Someone might well suggest here that God is able to bring down the high and the mighty by the means of the low and the frail.

I believe that there's more to this matter of STRANGE DELIVERANCE. God uses these strange plagues and uses them in rapid succession, one following another, primarily because:

God Requires Unconditional Surrender!

God does not want a concession here or a concession there. God wants unconditional surrender. And you have to watch Pharaoh because Pharaoh will pretend that he's had a change of heart. Let a plague settle on him and it looked like Pharaoh had religion. Let a little riot break out in southcentral L.A. (I mean, southcentral Goshen!) and Pharaoh starts talking about his conversion experience. But God keeps on sending plagues because he requires unconditional surrender. God does not require for his people the indignity of welfare or the insult of minimum wage. God wants Pharaoh's heart to change, and that requires unconditional surrender.

God is not going to settle for a project over here and a program over there; God's not interested in our set-asides and cutbacks and take-backs.

In this conflict there are some things that are nonnegotiable. Freedom, justice in our courts, the removal of illicit drugs and semiautomatic weapons, and liquor stores on every corner—they are all nonnegotiable. What God wants is for Pharaoh to change the system, and that requires unconditional surrender.

There is another reason for these plagues that usher in this STRANGE DELIVERANCE. God sends his plagues one after another in order that when the plagues are over

You Won't Forget Who Did It!

If you pay attention only to the frogs, the lice, and the flies you will misunderstand the meaning of the message. It's not what the frogs did, it's what God did. It's not what Moses did, it's what God did. The plagues are the instrument but God is the power.

God keeps on sending plagues over and over again because he requires UNCONDITIONAL SURRENDER, in order that you WON'T FORGET WHO DID IT, but he also sends them to let us know that he will deliver

By Any Means Necessary!

I know Malcolm said it but I'm more concerned about the fact that God did it BY ANY MEANS NECESSARY. Pharaoh and his magicians did everything they could but when they ran out of resources God still had power in his hand. Pharaoh has taken his best shot. I stand in the prophetic train of a Martin King today just to tell you that Pharaoh and the satanic systems of this world would have done all they can to destroy us: They have killed us, lynched us, mutilated us, raped us, castrated us, sent rabid dogs for us, fire-hosed us, miseducated us, strung us out on dope, killed our babies, locked us up in prisons, broken up our families, broken up our homes, called us out of our names, and have used every lethal weapon at their disposal.

But what they didn't count on was that God had frogs, and when his frogs ran out He had some lice, and when his lice ran out He had some hail, and when he ran out of hail He had some locusts. The message is clear: God will bring down the mighty by any means necessary!

God sends his plagues in swift succession, one following the other, just to remind us that

God Is Not Through Yet!

Deliverance is not complete. God could have sent one plague and one would have been enough. But God is not through yet. The pharaohs of this world, the agents of Satan, and the hounds of hell keep on coming back. The work is not yet done. There are children to educate, schools to build, addicts to be redeemed, the homeless sheltered, the hungry fed, the lost found, the left-out included. God keeps coming back—over and over again—because his redemptive work is yet in process.

Perhaps now we will hear Martin King, who declared, "Human progress never rolls in on the wheels of inevitability. It comes through the tireless efforts and the persistent work of dedicated individuals." We must become the agents of liberation. We must find again the "strength to love." The government can create programs for our people but we must turn again to an ethic of love and respect. We must become the frogs of freedom that get in Pharaoh's bed. We must become the lice of liberty that get under Pharaoh's skin. We must become the boils of persistent agitation to get on Pharaoh's mind. We must become the locusts of liberation that turn Pharaoh's sunlight into midnight. God is not through yet. And as long as God's not through, we're not through!

It is in the nature of God to deliver those who are oppressed. But we must not forget that his deliverance is not complete until there is blood on the doorpost. You remember that night when the Death Angel would come upon the children of Egypt, God sent word to Moses to tell the children of Israel to take the blood of the lamb and spread it on the two side posts and on the upper door-posts of their houses. God said, "I will pass through the land of Egypt this night and will smite all the firstborn in the land of Egypt. But the blood, when I see the blood on your doorpost, I will pass over you and the plague shall not be upon you to destroy you, when I smite the land of Egypt."

Our survival as a people requires blood on our doorpost. The blood of sacrifice. The blood of a life given to the pursuit of justice. The blood of a life committed to freedom. The blood of a life fit to live because you were willing to die. The blood that signs your name in the Lamb's Book of Life.

It may be STRANGE DELIVERANCE but I will not worry about the pharaohs of this land. I am covered by the blood. The slaves sang out one day:

"Done made my vow to the Lord,
And I never will turn back.
I will go, I shall go,
To see what the end will be."

I am covered by the blood. What started out as blood in the Nile stopped by long enough to put blood on my doorpost and then made its journey all the way to Calvary. I am covered by the blood.

The world may design my death but I am covered by the blood.

Do you know this blood? My ancestors said it was the blood "that signed my name"! I am covered by the blood.

It reaches to the highest mountain. It flows to the deepest valley. I am covered by the blood.

There is a fountain filled with blood,
Drawn from Immanuel's veins.

And sinners plunged beneath that flood,
Lose all their guilt stains!

E'er since by faith I saw the stream
Thy flowing wounds supply,
Redeeming love has been my theme,
And shall be till I die!

When this poor lisping stammering tongue
Lies silent in the grave,
Then in a nobler, sweeter song
I'll sing Thy power to save!

And that is

Strange Deliverance!

STEWARDS OF THE MYSTERIES
William Augustus Jones, Jr.

*In a message for all of us, but especially for preachers, this
sermon reminds us that no matter how others may define us,
we are ultimately defined by our relationship to God.
Preachers are not owners of the Word;
they are servants of God.*

1 CORINTHIANS 4:1–2

"Let a man so account to us, as of the ministers of Christ, and stewards of the mysteries of God. Moreover, it is required in stewards that a man be found faithful."

THE PREACHER SHOULD constantly examine and evaluate his calling. Any man commissioned by Christ to publish glad tidings ought to continually subject himself to serious scrutiny. Inner dialogue is an indispensable ingredient for the proper proclamation of redemption's story.

In order to preach, a man must have the courage to argue with himself. He must erect in his own being a table of dialogue and debate, where honesty and humility control the proceedings. I say this because no other person in the body politic is subject to so many pressures, pulled in so many directions, and buffeted by so many winds. The preacher is up there, open and exposed, confronted and challenged, tempted and tried. The very nature of human society makes it easy for him to be improperly swayed—if the inner dialogue is not kept current.

Of all the temptations and allurements that visit the preacher, there is none so sweet and so sweeping as the desire to be successful. We've been told that "nothing succeeds like success." The cultural climate is success-oriented. Men are measured by the miles they climb and the rate of speed at which they make the ascent. And the pulpit is victim of this societal pressure. This awareness gripped my head and heart a few years ago. It happened at a religious convocation. As I moved through the halls and among the people, I was pleased to know that nearly everybody there knew William A. Jones. Pride welled up in me whenever I heard people whispering, "There goes Dr. Jones of Brooklyn." I was made to feel that I was some kind of success symbol. "There goes Jones, pastor of Bethany in Brooklyn, well-known preacher, Christian activist."

But in a quiet moment in my room, I began to ponder the popularity problem. I began to scrutinize and weigh the matter, and I was hit squarely in the face with the stark reality that even the church is success-oriented. We're also caught up in the business of comparing, rating, and judging. There is competition, conscious and unconscious, between churches and preachers. Success is measured by size. Decisions are influenced not by what is said but by who says it. Truth is determined not by the facts presented but by the popularity quotient.

There in the creative aloneness of my room, in the midst of the inner dialogue, I was made to see clearly that it's quite easy, too easy, for we preachers to forget whose we are and who we are and what we're supposed to be about. The big-church syndrome can cause us to mistake numbers for members—to count heads instead of weighing hearts. Every church, Bethany included, has many more names than members. But we preachers are often guilty of playing the numbers game. We succumb to the success mythology. And the only way out of this sickening syndrome is to keep one's feet on the ground—to enter daily the inner sanction of self-scrutiny where we stand naked before the Holy Presence and let God check us out. And whenever we let God speak, He says in language unmistakably clear, "Preacher, what has happened to you? How could you set sail on the troubled sea of success motivation? Preacher, when I stirred your immortal spirit, handed you your calling and gave you your commission, I did not speak in terms of success. Preacher, I did not tell you to be successful. I told you simply to be faithful—'Be thou faithful unto death.'"

Paul is, without question, history's preacher prototype. After he initially went through the agony of acceptance, the same people who at first were reluctant to acknowledge his apostleship went to the other extreme. They lifted him to such a lofty elevation, to such a peak place, that the next act would have called for an expansion of the Trinity. The man who before had to feverishly explain and defend his credentials now had to passionately point out his basic humanity.

People have a proclivity for either putting you down or putting you up. It's either too low or too high. They make you either nothing or everything. At Corinth, the Christians who at first were hypercritical became too high in their praise. And Paul had to shake them out of that foolish posture by saying with utter candor, "To me was given a thorn in the flesh." And I sense the same instructive spirit at work when he tells the same crowd and us, "We are stewards of the mysteries of God. Let a man so account to us, as ministers of Christ and stewards of the mysteries of God."

Now that undercuts arrogance. It punctures pride. It disallows self-sufficiency. It underscores and punctuates the actuality and activity of mysteries from beyond ourselves. And the mysteries are not of our making. They belong to another, to One whose sovereignty is without challenge, to One whose domain extends beyond the perimeters of earth and sky, to One whose sweep is from everlasting to everlasting. They belong to him who is the Ancient of Days and who sitteth on the throne in glory. The mysteries are not ours. They're simply entrusted to us. They belong to the God of glory who presented us his self-portrait in the field preacher from Galilee. "We have this treasure in earthen vessels," but it's not our treasure. God loans it to us to cultivate and nurture, but never to own.

We are stewards of God's mysteries. But in our strivings to receive the fleeting, ephemeral plaudits of men, we sometimes act as owners rather than stewards. Success transcends faithfulness. The ego swells. The chest expands. Pride and presumption take possession of head and heart. And we begin to think in terms of what we've done for God instead of what God hath done through us. But the mysteries belong to Him! His is the power and His is the glory! The excellency of the power is not of us, but of God!

Recently I witnessed an example of this truth, an example so vivid it was frightening. (It's always frightening when God comes close enough to show men that the mysteries belong to Him.) I heard two men preach to the same people in the same place on the same day. One man was tall, handsome, imposing, and impressive. He had what we call charisma. His words were well-chosen. His nouns were proper, his adjectives descriptive. His sentences were as smooth as molten lava. We listened, but nothing happened. The

Spirit did not descend and make that moving march from heart to heart and from breast to breast. He spoke with great eloquence — but nothing happened. Now, the other man had no pulpit presence, no comeliness. He was relatively short in stature, his body was misshapen, his attire untailored and unfashionable. Most people would describe him as unattractive. But as he began to wrestle with the mysteries, something happened. As he preached, you just knew that he was leaning and depending on the Lord. As he preached, you experienced the Holy Presence. As he preached, you felt that you weren't really looking at him. You didn't see the vessel; you saw the treasure. You didn't see him; you saw Jesus. The luminous glow of the divine enveloped his person. The Spirit started walking all over the place. The Holy Ghost was in the air, in the light, on our faces, and in our hearts.

And I knew once more that preaching is more than a certain physique, more than some words wrapped around a text. Preaching is what God does with a ready tongue. It's a journey from the finite to the infinite and back again. It's the condensation of eternity into the fleeting moments of passing experience. It's a divine symphony played on the instrument of a human tongue. It's the leading of men to a collision with reality. It's God's instrument for breaking the hard heart and healing the broken heart.

Preaching is that certain Presence, that awesome power — that rapture that comes in from outside ourselves. And nothing can happen unless and until the Spirit comes. God's got to breathe on it. God's got to bless it. That's what our fathers and mothers meant when they sang:

Come by here, my Lord, Come by here;
Come by here, my Lord, Come by here;
Come by here, my Lord, Come by here;
O Lord, Come by here.

Somebody needs you, Lord, Come by here;
Somebody needs you, Lord, Come by here;
Somebody needs you, Lord, Come by here;
O Lord, Come by here.

Nothing can happen, unless and until the Spirit comes. The mysteries are not ours. We are stewards of His mysteries.

Now, a steward is a manager of the assets and affairs of another. His is a work of trust and responsibility. He didn't make that which he manages. He's just the manager. But management connotes accountability. The steward is accountable to the owner. We who are stewards of God's mysteries must give account to God. God Himself is the sole judge of our stewardship.

Paul makes it plain in this passage to whom judgment belongs. He says, "With me it is a very small thing that I should be judged of you, or of man's judgment. You Corinthians are prone to pass judgment on my work, but your judgment is light stuff. Your judgment doesn't disturb me at all. In fact, I don't even take time to try to judge myself. You Corinthians are not qualified to judge me. I'm not qualified to judge myself. The only qualified judge is the One to whom the mysteries belong. He that judgeth me is the Lord."

Now, I'm appreciative of this. I'm glad it's this way. For you see, if I'm judged by you, your appraisal will of necessity be incorrect. My friends will minimize my faults and maximize my virtues. My enemies will minimize my virtues and maximize my faults. Why, after nearly twenty-seven years in Bethany Church, there are some souls who have not yet decided that I'm a pretty good pastor. Perhaps there are some who've concluded that I'll never be their kind of pastor. On the other hand, there are those who in their praise ignore my shortcomings. Even I myself am incapable of judging my work. I may think I've done a fairly good job, but an affirmative answer is the prerogative of God alone.

I do know that according to the success mythology, there are some areas in which I've failed. I know and openly confess that in some ways I've come up terribly short. There are a lot of people whose lives I haven't been able to touch. I've failed to motivate many to a genuine stewardship. There are eyes I have not opened to the mysteries of God. I've tried, but in many instances I've failed. And the only thing that gives me hope and keeps me from despairing is the knowledge that the Kingdom is not evaluated by human standards of success. In the Kingdom, the order is: "Be faithful."

You see, our faith declares that in God's service, in the Kingdom's work, in the Owner's vineyard, you can be faithful and yet seem to fail. According to the world's way of judging, you can fail in your faithfulness.

Help me out, Moses. I see Moses departing the burning bush with a burning desire — on fire on the inside, filled with godly passion, captured by liberation's dream, and inspired by the hope of a Promised Land. He approaches Pharaoh's throne and with the rod of God in his right hand declares with authority from heaven, "Pharaoh, let my people go!" Pharaoh's hard-heartedness produces seven plagues. Moses leads Israel out of Egypt by night and a miracle is wrought at the swirling waters of the Red Sea. But a liberated people begins to complain, and a forty-day journey is lengthened to forty years. It looks like Moses is a failure, but one day out on Pisgah, after many years' marchings, I hear God tell Moses to come up and get a view of Canaan from Dan to Beersheba — and up there in that summit, God rocked his body to sleep in the arms of death, and placed his soul in Paradise.

Paul, you come and help me. I see you in your last days. You're under house arrest in the city of Rome. You're a prisoner of Nero. Your pilgrimage from Damascus to Jerusalem has been a rough journey on a rocky road. You've known beatings and stripes. You've been in all kinds of perils. You've been shipwrecked and storm-tossed. And now, you await a terrible execution on Nero's chopping block. Paul, it looks like you're a failure. But I hear him say, "I am now ready to be offered, and the time of my departure is at hand. I have fought a good fight, I have finished my course, I have kept the faith. Henceforth, there is laid up for me a crown of righteousness, which the Lord, the righteous judge, shall give me that day."

I'm now looking at another. Jesus is his name. Now Jesus, my master, you come and help me. I see you departing the regal splendor of your father's house. You left the throne in glory. You were born in a barn in Bethlehem. To escape Herod's evil, you had to flee into Egypt. You grew up in a ghetto. When you started your redemptive work, your own people rejected you. You were never able to keep a crowd. You fed five thousand and they walked away. The Pharisees hated you. The Sadducees despised you. The powers that be considered you a threat. Before the Last Supper, you had twelve men. After the Supper, you had eleven. And of that number, one denied you, one doubted you, and the rest, save one, forsook you and fled. You were tried in two courts. You were lied on and spat upon. They sentenced you to death on a cross. They put a crown of thorns on your head; they thrust a spear in your side. You died amidst the mockery of cursing men. Satan shouted, demons danced; hell got happy! Pharisees were pleased. Sadducees were satisfied. In the eyes of men, you failed, Jesus.

But early Sunday morning, in the golden splendor of a Sunday sunrise, I hear a shaking in a grave. I hear the breaking of the fetters of death. I hear a rumbling that sounds like a divine disturbance. And I see that figure who died on Calvary stand up and march forth in Resurrection glory. And I hear him say to the Patmos prisoner, "Behold, I am he that was dead. But now I'm alive forevermore."

Oh, if you're faithful, the righteous judge will have the last sayso. The world will sometimes brand you a failure, but if you're faithful—if you keep on toiling through the storm and rain; if you hang in and hold on—he who knows how to judge, he who knows the hairs on your head, and the nature of your heart, he'll say, "Well done."

I know what it is to be buffeted and battered. I know what it is to be 'buked and scorned. I know what it is to be misunderstood and even maligned. I know what it is to be tossed and driven on the restless sea of time. I know what it is, and how it feels, to do your best and then be condemned. I know what it means to be faithful and then be branded a failure.

But I remember, thank God, that I'm a steward of his mysteries. God is my boss. God is my judge. I'm his steward. I'm his servant. I'm working for the King. I'm on the battlefield for my Lord. And it pleases me to know that —

If when you give the best of your service,
Telling the world that the Savior is come,

Be not dismayed when men don't believe you,
He'll understand and say well done.

It suits my heart to know that —

If when you try and fail in your trying,
Hands sore and scarred, from the work you've begun,
Just take up your cross, run quickly to meet Him,
He'll understand and say well done.

Oh when I come, to the end of my journey,
Weary of life, and the battle is won,
Carrying the staff, and cross of redemption,
He'll understand and say well done!

If you're faithful, you may seem to fail — but there's no way to lose.
You're a winner — in life and in death.

GOD IS FAITHFUL
WHEN WE FAIL
Harold Dean Trulear

*Through the deep and troubling depression of prophet
Elijah we are taught that God remains loving and
faithful to us even when we are unsuccessful or
believe ourselves to be failures.*

1 KINGS 17–19

I WANT TO call your attention on this Lord's day to 1 Kings 19:1–4:

> And Ahab told Jezebel all that Elijah had done, and withal how he had slain all the prophets with the sword. Then Jezebel sent a messenger unto Elijah, saying, So let the Gods do to me and more also, if I make not thy life as one of them by to morrow about this time.

Translation: "I'm gonna kill you." That's what she said to him. "I'm gonna kill you. You're goin' down, Elijah, you're goin' down."

> When he saw that, he arose, and went for his life, and came to Beer-sheba, which belongeth to Judah, and left his servant there. But he himself went a day's journey into the wilderness, and came and sat down under a juniper tree; and he requested for himself that he might die, and said, It is enough; now, O Lord, take away my life; for I am not better than my fathers.

He is faithful when we fail.
That's what I want to talk about for the next few moments.
He's faithful when we fail.
Who is this Elijah, this man who comes into our presence today by way of Holy Scripture? Who is he? By looking at him in this passage we would think that he is a coward. By looking at him in this passage we would think ill of him, for when his enemies, the enemies of God, told him that they would try to take his life for standing up for God, he does the cowardly thing: He runs off into the wilderness and asks God to take his life. But, if you were to look at the pages of 1 Kings 17 and 18 and see what this man did, you would get a totally different picture. This is the man who walked into King Ahab's palace without an appointment, got past the secretary, got through the armed guards, stood before the

throne of the King of Israel, and said, "As the Lord God of Israel lives before whom I stand, there shall be no dew, no rain these years except according to my word."[13] This is the man who went down to the brook at Cherith and without any visible means of support, without any refrigerator or any food store, without food stamps or welfare, he just sat down by the brook and trusted God to feed him twice a day. This is the man who went down to a widow's house in Zarephath, and all she had in the refrigerator was just a little Hostess Twinkie—a little cupcake—some olive oil, and not enough to feed herself and her son. He said to her, if you let me have the Twinkie, God will feed you with a banquet. This is the man who a few days later stretched himself out over this woman's son after he had died and brought him back to life. That's this man, Elijah.

In chapter 18, he challenges the prophets of Baal to see whose God is really the Lord—450 prophets of Baal prophesizing under their false god, trying to get him to bring fire down from heaven and consume a sacrifice. Elijah is so sure of his god that he laughs at the other fellows. Have you ever laughed at the devil? Have you ever just laughed at the enemy? Some of us say, I got too much respect for the Devil to laugh at him. I don't have enough confidence. Elijah had so much confidence in God that he could laugh at the Devil and his minions. He made fun of them as they ran around trying to sacrifice to this false god. He says, Maybe your god has gone on a vacation. In King James it says, maybe he has gone *aside*. That's a polite way of saying maybe your god is in the bathroom. That's how much confidence he had in God.

And then when he went to pray to God to send fire down to consume the sacrifice, before the words even left Elijah's lips, the fire came down and consumed the sacrifice, demonstrating that Elijah's god was the true God. I call that a man of faith—so much faith that when James was looking for an example of a praying man, he says Elijah is a praying man. A man who had such prophetic boldness that when God himself needed a representative for the whole school of the prophets in the Old Testament to stand with Jesus on the mountain of transfiguration, with Moses representing the law, he sent Elijah down to stand with Jesus.[14] A man of such great and gifted and anointed oratory that when John the Baptist showed up and began proclaiming the Kingdom of God and repentance, some folk thought Elijah had come back.[15] And now Queen Jezebel says, Elijah, I'm gonna take care of you. You took care of my prophets, I'm gonna off you. That's what we used to say when I was coming up.

And all of a sudden, the man of God—the one who God takes in a fiery chariot in just a few years—this man of God, who is a prophet's prophet, runs scared. We used to say "like a chump." The rap kids say, "He became a track star."

And he ran. He ran when the challenge came.

The Bible says that he ran into the wilderness—ran for his life. He goes into the wilderness and he sits down under a juniper tree and says, Lord, it's enough. Take away my life. I just can't take it anymore. Have you ever said that? When I was a little kid, I used to watch Popeye and he said it this way: "I had all I can stands and I can't stands no more." Have you ever been there? You know something about that, don't you? I know you don't want to admit that in church. I know you really want to pretend that you are always living holy. You want to pretend that every day is Sunday. I know you want to put on that church face. I know you want everybody to think that when trouble comes all you do is call on the Lord and he just wipes the trouble away. But every now and then, I don't know about you, I get like Elijah. I say, Lord, I can't take it. Lord, if heaven is better than this, then maybe I oughta check it out now.

I guess this passage is here so we won't think too highly of Elijah. So that even when we have sweet success, we know that there are times in our lives when we are going to get depressed. There are times in our lives when we are still going to feel like giving up. We've had great success. The Lord has brought us from a mighty long way. God has brought you from so far that it is almost unbelievable. And you feel that because God has brought you so far that now you're not going to have any more trouble and all of a sudden Satan hits you with something. You say, I thought this stuff was over when I got saved. I had got saved, I'm in the church, I'm praising his holy name, and now the opposition is still there. Somebody once said, "It wasn't this bad before I got saved."

Here is Elijah in the same situation as you. Lord, it is enough. Take away my life, for I am no better than my fathers. He had failed at this point. Don't think that the word hadn't gotten out. Elijah had just overseen the killing of 450 false prophets. You know that was in the news, that when Elijah turned into a chump, they put that in the paper. "Prophet Becomes Punk." Sounds like the *Post*, doesn't it?

You know that it was on talk radio in Israel. They said, Oh yeah, he was such a great man of God. If he were such a great man of God he'd stand up in a situation like this. You know that some of the people who stuck with him when he was being successful, they turned their backs on him. In fact, when we find him in the wilderness, he's all by himself. Is there a word from the Lord for Elijah? Is there a presence of God? Is there something that God gives to this man in the midst of his failure? I want to suggest to you that God does take care of Elijah. And that God takes care of you and me. He is faithful even when we fail. Even when we let him down. Even when we let ourselves down. Even when we let our friends and loved ones down. God is still faithful to us.

When you gave your life to Christ, God said, I will be faithful to you no matter what. No matter how low you sink, no matter how many mistakes you make, I'll still be faithful to you. And I'll do whatever it takes to bring you back. I'll do whatever it takes to re- store you. I'll do whatever it takes to build you up. And that's what God does for Elijah. That's covenant love. It means that God, because of His love for us, had made a covenant with us. It means that the whole thing depends on Him. I know we like to talk about how we hold God's unchanging hand, but the truth is that God takes care of us.

I live on a very busy street and I have three small children — six, eight, and eleven. It's the busiest street, Highway 13, running through my county. And when it's time to cross the street, I have to take them by the hand to take them across. And when we get to the other side of the street, my daughter will look up at me and say, Daddy, it's a good thing we held on to you. My daughter doesn't realize she wasn't doing the holding. If she tried to let go, I still had hold of her. She didn't get across the street because she was holding onto Daddy's hand. No, no. She got across the street 'cause Daddy wouldn't let go of his child. And in this way God shows up for Elijah.

There are four things that God gives to this prophet's prophet in the midst of his misery, as he says, It is enough; I had all I can stand; I'm ready to die. The first thing He does is, He sends an angel to him and gives him permission to take care of himself. The Bible says that as he lay and slept under the juniper tree an angel touched him and said *"Arise and eat."*[16] He got permission to take care of himself. Now, you're looking at me funny. What am I talking about? We, as Christians, are so often challenged to bear one another's burdens in the heat of the day. As Christians, we are compelled to love one another and take care of one another and sometimes we spend so much time taking care of everybody else that we stop taking care of ourselves. If you're a parent, you need to hear me today. We spend so much time taking care of our children—we put so much into our children—we lose sight of the things we need for ourselves. Then we get worn down. We get tired out. We get broken down and then we're of no use to anybody. What God is saying to Elijah is, Elijah, you been taking care of everybody else. You been preaching to everybody else. You been working with everybody else. Take time. Take a vacation. Take a break. Get some rest. Read a good book. Look at some TV. Spend some time in prayer. Eat something you like. Spoil yourself. Buy something you been denying yourself. Take care of yourself. You've been denying yourself. I'm not telling you to go take all of your money and go to Bermuda or something like that. You know what I'm saying.

Elijah, *Arise and eat.* The journey is too great for you. You've been in a mode of helping others for so long. He says you have permission to take care of yourself. Because if you don't take care of yourself, you won't be around to take care of anyone else.

The second thing God does for Elijah is, He pauses to hear. We always think about how God hears us, and no one would deny that He does. But I want you to consider what it meant for God to pause and hear Elijah as he's talking, because Elijah is saying some really deep stuff. He says, Lord, take away my life. It is enough. I am no better than my fathers. He's saying, I give up. God even listens to us when we give up. God understands that sometimes we talk contrary to our faith walks. God wants you to be honest with Him. And sometimes you just don't feel like anything. Sometimes you get upset. You ever get angry with God? We're afraid to tell God that we're angry because we have so much respect for the Lord. But you know what? The Lord already knows you're angry with him. He knows your heart. God wants us to come to him honestly and tell him where we're struggling. Somebody says it's so negative. But you know what? God can take your negative and turn it into a positive. Look at Elijah talking about it is enough; take away my life. He says, I want to die. He didn't really want to die. If he really wanted to die all he had to do was stay where he was—Jezebel would have taken care of him. He didn't want to die. God is so awesome He could look past the foolishness of your lips and see the problem of your heart.

You know what? Even when you give up, you didn't give up. It takes faith to say, I give up. You're looking at me funny. I was driving down the street one day and I was so upset with God. The Lord had told me to do something; I knew it was right. I knew it was the thing the Lord wanted me to do. And I was so mad at God. I said, Lord, I can't do it. In fact, I don't believe in you anymore. I did. I was teaching in the seminary and I drove down the street and the Lord spoke to me. He doesn't speak to me very often, but sometimes the Lord speaks to me, and speaks to you, too. Sometimes you just hear His voice. You know what God said to me? *If you don't believe in me, who are you talking to?*

You know, if you tell God that you give up, that means you had enough faith to believe he heard you when you said it. If you tell God, I can't take it anymore, it means you had enough faith to believe he heard you when you said you couldn't take it.

So, even when Elijah is ready to give up and he says, I don't have anything left, God says, Yes you do. Because if you didn't have anything left, you couldn't have said that. If you didn't have anything left, you wouldn't have asked me to take away your life.

If you didn't have anything left, you would have stayed there and let Jezebel do it. But there is still some faith in you. You're talking about giving up. You feel like giving up. But there is still some faith in you. I put it in you when you gave your life to my son. I put it in you when you confessed Christ the Savior. I put it in you when you joined the church. I put it in you and I am not taking it out. You feel like giving up, but I am telling you there is still faith in you.

The third thing He does is give Elijah His presence in a new way. The Bible says that He then tells Elijah, Come on up into the mountain. When Elijah went up into the mountain, a strong wind passed by. And when Elijah was up in the mountain, there was a great earthquake. And when Elijah was up in the mountain, there was great fire. But God was not to be found in the earthquake, the wind, or the fire. Elijah was accustomed to an earthquake God. He had seen God shake things up before. When the earthquake came by, God said, No, no, I'm not in that. He had seen God come in the fire before. In chapter 18, he saw God come down out of Mount Carmel to consume the sacrifice. He had seen God come like fire before. He had seen God come like wind before. He saw Him blow the breath of life into the widow's son at Zarephath. He had seen the wind before, but now God was coming to him in a new way. Coming to him in a still, small voice.

You know some of us think that if it ain't loud it ain't God. If the preacher doesn't holler, God ain't spoke. If the choir ain't loud and folk ain't falling out all over the place then the Lord ain't spoke. I like to shout and I like it when it's loud, but sometimes God speaks when it's quiet. Sometimes God speaks in a still, small voice: Elijah, I know you would like to have it like the earthquake, but I want you to experience me in a new way. Elijah, I know you would like to have it like the fire, but I want you to see me in a new way. I know that you're used to seeing me like the wind, but I want you to see me when it's quiet. Have you talked to God in the quiet lately? When there was nobody to say amen to your prayer? When there was nobody to clap hands while you sang? When there was nobody to accompany you on the organ or the drums? Just by yourself, in the quiet?

Elijah, I want to show you something new and different; I want to expand your consciousness. God is speaking in the still, small voice of calm to your spirit. He gives him his presence in a new way.

And then if that's not enough, Elijah is still complaining: I'm the only one left. I thank you for the new presence, but you don't know how lonely it is. Thank you for permission to take care of myself. I appreciate being able to eat and take this vacation, but I still feel so lonely. Lord, thank you for pausing to hear me as I talk to you out of the misery of my soul, but I still feel lonely. God says to him, Elijah, I still got seven thousand that have not bowed their knees to Baal. He gives him some people to surround him with faith. That's why we come to church on Sunday morning. I know you can get what you want off the TV preachers and I know you can get the songs off the radio. But there is nothing like coming together in the body of Christ. Elijah, you feel alone, but if you look to the left of you and look to the right of you, there is somebody who is dealing with something just as difficult as you. Elijah, I know you feel like you're all by yourself, but if you look you're surrounded by folks who have come on up the rough side of the mountain. Elijah, I know you feel like you're all by yourself. I'm gonna surround you with people who will pray for you, people who know about the struggle. People who have a testimony about how God brought them over in difficult times. I'm gonna surround you with a people who have the testimony about a God who changes mountains into monuments. I've got seven thousand, says God, who have not bowed their knees to Baal.

Oh, God is faithful when we fail. He gives us permission to take care of ourselves. He pauses to hear us even when our prayers don't make sense. He gives us his presence in a new way and gives us people to support us in our journey.

I am reminded, in closing, about a story told by a pastor that I know. He had been a pastor of one of the great churches in upstate New York. He all of a sudden came down with a condition that we now know to be manic depression. Manic depression is a condition that is chemical in nature. Therefore, the person gets so depressed that no matter what you do they can't seem to snap out of it. And that brother was so depressed that he resigned from pastoring his church. The deacons came by to read prayers to him, but he said you can read all the prayers you want, I don't feel like going to church. Then some of the sisters would come by and say let's sing some of the Lord's songs together. He said you can sing all you want, I just don't feel like singing. Some of the other preachers formed an association and would come by and say let's read Scripture together, Brother Pastor. He would say, I don't feel like reading Scripture. You read the Bible all you want, I just don't feel like it.

Then after three years of dealing with this condition, he woke up one morning and all of a sudden the depression had lifted from him. God had taken away that cloud from over his head and all the joy of the Lord was once again his strength. He went back into the pulpit and began declaring how God had brought him through. He went and gave his testimony all over, saying that even manic depression could not defeat him. And one day he was giving his testimony in a church in Connecticut, and a woman came up to him and shook his hand and she said, "Brother, I think that it is so marvelous that even in the midst of your depression you held to God's unchanging hand." And the preacher said, "Lady, you didn't hear a word I said. I just told you that for three years, I wouldn't go to church. For three years, I couldn't read the Bible. For three years, I didn't sing God's songs. For three years, I didn't pray to God. Lady, I didn't hold to God's hand; God held on to my hand." And that's the good news for you and me today: When we're weak He'll hold your hand.

ENDNOTES

[1]Robert Browning, "Epilogue," *Masterpieces of Religious Verse* (New York: Harper & Row, 1948), 578.

[2]Harriet du Autermont, "Some Faith at Any Cost," *Masterpieces of Religious Verse* (New York: Harper & Row, 1948), 306.

[3]James Russell Lowell, "L'Envoi to the Muse," *The Complete Poetical Works of James Russell Lowell*, Cambridge Edition (Boston: Houghton Mifflin, 1896), 347–48.

[4]Ralph Waldo Emerson, "Forerunners," *Great Poems of the English Language* (New York: Tudor Publishing, 1935), 663.

[5]Louis Untermeyer, "Prayer," *Long Feud: Selected Poems* (New York: Harcourt Brace Jovanovich, 1962).

[6]Clive Samson, "The Rich Young Ruler," *The Witnesses, and Other Poems* (London: Methuen, 1956).

[7]Adam Clayton Powell, Jr., *Adam by Adam: The Autobiography of Adam Clayton Powell, Jr.* (New York: Dial Press, 1971), 34–35.

[8]William Meyers, *The Irresistible Urge to Preach* (Atlanta: Aaron Press, 1992), 58.

[9]*Ibid.*

[10]Rev. Preston Washington, audiocassette of testimony given at the National Call to Dialogue: "What does It Mean to be Black and Christian?" Nashville, Vanderbilt University, 1992.

[11]"The African-American Male," theme paper presented to the National Black Catholic Congress Foundation, Baltimore, 1991.

[12]*Ibid.*

[13]1 Kings 17:1 (King James Version).

[14]Mark 9:12.

[15]Matthew 17:10–13.

[16]1 Kings 19:5 (King James Version).

AUTHOR BIOGRAPHIES

REVEREND SAMUEL D. PROCTOR

Dr. Samuel D. Proctor is Pastor Emeritus of the Abyssinian Baptist Church in Harlem, and served as director of the Peace Corps under President John F. Kennedy. He is professor of education, Graduate School of Education (Martin Luther King Memorial Chair), Rutgers University, and has served as president of Virginia Union University and North Carolina A & T State University.

BENJAMIN E. MAYS (1895–1984)

An ordained Baptist minister, Benjamin Mays served as president of Morehouse College in Atlanta for many years and influenced legions of African-American male students, including Martin Luther King, Jr. Born in South Carolina, he earned his Ph.D. from the University of Chicago and was the recipient of honorary degrees from colleges and universities in the United States as well as in Africa. Throughout his life, Dr. Mays served as a dignified and distinguished leader in the fight for equal justice through organizations such as the World Council of Churches and the YMCA, and also served as president of the Atlanta Board of Education. He authored several books, including *The Negro's God* (1938) and his autobiography *Born to Rebel* (1972).

GARDNER C. TAYLOR

Senior Pastor Emeritus of Concord Baptist Church of Christ, Brooklyn, New York, Gardner C. Taylor is widely regarded as one of the greatest preachers to ever enter a pulpit. He is a member of the Academy of Homiletics, and was named as one of the "Twelve Most Effective Preachers in the English Speaking World" in a 1996 Baylor University study. Dr. Taylor has influenced and inspired both clergy and parishioners all over the world and is the author of three books: *How Shall They Preach* (1977), *The Scarlet Thread* (1981), and *Chariots Aflame* (1988).

J. ALFRED SMITH, SR.

Dr. J. Alfred Smith is the senior pastor of the Allen Temple Baptist Church in Oakland, California, and professor of Christian ministry at the American Baptist Seminary of the West and the Graduate Theological Union at Berkeley. Dr. Smith is the past president of the American Baptist Churches of the West and the Progressive National Baptist Convention. He is a graduate of the Missouri School of Religion, American Baptist Seminary of the West, Golden Gate Baptist Theological Seminary, and Western Baptist College. Dr. Smith has authored sixteen books used by seminaries, Bible students, teachers, and scholars worldwide. He is the recipient of numerous community, statewide, and national awards.

HOWARD THURMAN (1900–1981)

Poet, mystic, philosopher, and theologian, Howard Thurman was the foremost African-American spiritualist of his time. At the time of his passing in 1981, Dr. Thurman was dean emeritus of Marsh Chapel, Boston University, and chairman of the board of trustees of the Howard Thurman Educational Trust in San Francisco. An ordained Baptist minister, Dr. Thurman also served as dean of Rankin Chapel, Howard University; professor at Howard University School of Religion; and director of religious life at Morehouse and Spelman colleges in Atlanta. He was founder of the Church for the Fellowship of All Peoples in San Francisco, the first interracial, interdenominational church in the United States and also served as honorary canon of the Cathedral of Saint John the Divine in New York City. Dr. Thurman authored more than twenty books, including *Meditations of the Heart, Jesus and the Disinherited,* and *The Inward Journey.*

A. SAFIYAH FOSUA

Dr. A. Safiyah Fosua is a pastor, writer, educator, and missionary. Born in Kansas City, Kansas, she is a graduate of Northwestern University, Oral Roberts Seminary, and United Theological Seminary. She is an ordained minister of the Iowa Annual Conference of United Methodists and has pastored several churches. In the spring of 1996, she departed for Ghana, where, along with her husband, Dr. Kwasi Kena, she will serve a three-year term as an instructor at the Freeman Bible College in Kumasi. Dr. Fosua is the author of *Mother Wit: 365 Devotionals for African-American Women.*

RAYMOND LEE HARRIS, JR.

Rev. Raymond Harris is a graduate of Princeton University and St. Mary's Seminary and University in Baltimore. He was the third African American to be ordained for the priesthood in the history of the Archdiocese of Baltimore. He serves as an associate pastor at St. Anthony of Padua/Most Precious Blood Faith Community, where he focuses on issues such as parish-community relations, African-American involvement in the life of the church, and the community, youth ministry, and adult religious education.

H. BEECHER HICKS, JR.

Dr. H. Beecher Hicks, senior minister of the Metropolitan Baptist Church in Washington, D.C., is a graduate of the University of Arkansas and Colgate Rochester Divinity School. President of Martin Luther King Fellows, Inc., he was named by *Ebony* magazine as one of the fifteen greatest African-American preachers. Dr. Hicks is the author of *Images of the Black Preacher, Preaching Through a Storm,* and *Correspondence with a Cripple from Tarsus.* He is married to the former Elizabeth Harrison. They are the parents of H. Beecher III, Ivan Douglas, and Kristin Elizabeth.

WILLIAM AUGUSTUS JONES, JR.

Dr. William Jones has served as pastor of Bethany Baptist Church, Brooklyn, New York, since 1962. Educated at the University of Kentucky, Crozer Theological Seminary, and Colgate Rochester Divinity School, he has enjoyed a broad preaching ministry in the United States and abroad. A former president of the Progressive National Baptist Convention and founder of the National Black Pastors' Conference, he has been called "one of the great theologians and expository preachers in the country today." Dr. Jones has authored several books, including *Responsible Preaching* and *God in the Ghetto.*

HAROLD DEAN TRULEAR

Dr. Harold Trulear is professor of church and society at New York Theological Seminary. An alumnus of Morehouse College and Drew University, he has taught at Drew University and Eastern Baptist Theological Seminary. He has served several churches and currently serves as associate pastor of Community Baptist Church of Love in Paterson, New Jersey. Dr. Trulear is on the board of directors of InterVarsity Christian Fellowship and the New York Higher Education Consortium.

About the Editors

RHINOLD LAMAR PONDER

Rhinold Lamar Ponder, an attorney and literary agent, has taught African-American literature, politics, and law at Rutgers University, City University of New York (CUNY), and St. Peter's College in New Jersey, where he was the director of the black studies program. He has edited numerous publications, including the *NYU Review of Law and Social Change*, and his social commentary has appeared in the *New York Times*, *Miami Herald*, and the *City Sun*. A graduate of Princeton University, he achieved his J.D. at New York University Law School and his M.A. in journalism and M.S. in African-American studies from Boston University.

MICHELE TUCK-PONDER

Michele Tuck-Ponder is the mayor of Princeton Township, New Jersey. She has served as press secretary to Congressman Louis Stokes, special assistant to United States Senator Frank Lautenberg, assistant counsel to New Jersey Governor Jim Florio, deputy director of the New Jersey Division on Women, and assistant director of the New Jersey Division on Civil Rights. She earned a J.D. from the University of Pennsylvania Law School and a B.S. in journalism from Northwestern University. In 1990, she founded the New Jersey African-American Organ Donor Awareness Organization, and serves on a number of boards and commissions throughout the state of New Jersey.